GRATITUDE

Affirming
One Another
Through
Stories

"These stories reflect Len's keen insight, deep faith, and profound gratitude for a world gifted by God's mercy and love. In an economy where we are conditioned to always want more, it is life-giving and encouraging to find someone who is grateful for the really important things, most of which are gifts we can neither earn nor purchase. For one reason or another, Christians too often live out of a spirit of scarcity — always fearful that there is not enough love, mercy, forgiveness, or compassion to go around. Len's stories show us a deep and transforming appreciation for a spirit of abundance — a sure conviction that God's love is not limited by self-preservation, and God's mercy is not bounded by human justice. These are the stories to remember when we are confused about what really matters, or afraid that we have fallen too far short of God's expectations.

DAVE CUSHING
Director of Adult Formation, Catholic Parishes of Waterloo, Iowa

"*Gratitude.* What a perfect choice for a title. Len Froyen takes all the things of importance and weaves them into a single unity that reaches through all the threads of a life. He identifies all positions and all emotions of gentleness and a lack of aggression, and having identified who he is, he guides us to a like position."

DEAN SCHWARZ
internationally-acclaimed writer and designer

"Gratitude's descriptive stories brought back memories of cleaning cupboards beside my grandmother, walking elbow-to-elbow through high-school hallways, and reminiscing with cherished friends around a roaring campfire. Each memory flooded me with warmth as I reflected on them after reading these chapters.

"Gratitude shifts our focus to view each experience, past or present, through a spiritually-sharper lens. Froyen alerts us to the importance of searching for gratitude in the simple acts of shopping in the grocery story, waiting in the doctor's office, or walking around the block. After reading *Gratitude,* my heart awoke anticipating another day for which to be thankful.

"Froyen reminded me that each moment grants an opportunity to enrich life through the simple, yet profound, act of gratitude.

"As a director of adult faith formation, I highly recommend *Gratitude.* Froyen's stories, coupled with reflection activities and discussion starters, is the perfect springboard for individuals or groups to dive in and deepen their faith through the intentional practice of gratitude. With gratitude, each moment becomes gift and our lives become blessed. Thank you, Len, for blessing us with your wisdom on gratitude!"

MARY PEDERSON, D. MIN.
Director of Adult Faith Formation, Archdiocese of Dubuque

GRATITUDE

Affirming
One Another
Through
Stories

LEN FROYEN

Parkhurst Brothers Publishers

MARION, MICHIGAN

www.parkhurstbrothers.com

Parkhurst Brothers books are distributed to the trade through the Chicago Distribution Center, and may be ordered through Ingram Book Company, Baker & Taylor, Follett Library Resources and other book industry wholesalers. To order from Chicago Distribution Center, phone 800-621-2736 or send a fax to 800-621-8476. Copies of this and other Parkhurst Brothers, Inc., Publishers titles are available to organizations and corporations for purchase in quantity by contacting Special Sales Department at our home office location, listed on our website. Manuscript submission guidelines for this publishing company are available at our website.

Printed in the United States of America

First Edition, 2013

2013 2014 2015 2016 2017 2018   10 9 8 7 6 5 4 3 2 1

Library of Congress Cataloging-in-Publication Data:

Froyen, Len A.
 Gratitude : affirming one another through stories / Len Froyen. -- First Edition.
    pages cm
 ISBN 978-1-62491-019-7 -- ISBN 978-1-62491-020-3
 1. Gratitude--Anecdotes. 2. Storytelling. 3. Gratitude. I. Title.
 BJ1533.G8F76 2013
 241'.4--dc23

                     2013019781

ISBN: Trade Paperback 978-1-62491-019-7
ISBN: e-book 978-1-62491-020-3

COVER DESIGN: Wendell E. Hall
PAGE DESIGN: Shelly Culbertson
EDITORS: Carole Yates, Cheryl Smith
PROOFREADERS: Bill and Barbara Paddack
ACQUIRED FOR PARKHURST BROTHERS, INC., PUBLISHERS BY: Ted Parkhurst

112013

Dedicated to Gail,

my wife of fifty-five years,

who contributes daily to my growth in gratitude

and inspires me to share the gift with others.

Acknowledgements

Stories are time-honored inroads to telling and properly understanding our lives. They converge as the centerpiece for this book. I am grateful to members of my immediate and extended families who supplied the stories that taught me to stitch gratitude into the tapestry of my life. I am also grateful to Joel Schorn, who helped me clarify and consolidate my original thoughts about the content and format for this book. Likewise, the challenging insights of publisher Ted Parkhurst were helpful and encouraging throughout the final draft process. I am much indebted to Carole Yates, who began editing the book, and to Cheryl Smith, who ardently and meticulously read each line, and improved, simplified, and disposed of many of them. My appreciation to Lisa Geisler and Gary Froyen, who typed early versions of several chapters, and to Gail, who patiently and tediously typed multiple drafts of the manuscript. I am thankful for deacons and their wives in the Archdiocese of Dubuque, who helped me embark upon this journey as mentors and models of gratitude. And my thanks to the numerous persons who daily stand at the intersection of gratitude and happiness and invite me into the fruitful marriage of both.

Len Froyen
May 2013

Table of Contents

Preface

*"The object of my affection can change my complexion
from white to rosy red, anytime she holds my hand,
tells me that she is mine."*

TRUMAN "PINKY" TOMLIN, "The Object of My Affection"

These lyrics capture two distinguishing features of gratitude. Generally, we are grateful when we make something our own, whether it be an object, a person, or a condition. And when we do so, it gives us pleasure. Songs use music and words to tell us what we long to have and how we feel upon the realization of it. Likewise, books can put us in touch with gratitude. Beneath the words and the music are the tenor and the tenets of gratitude.

My primary purpose in writing this book is to make gratitude the object of your affection and a pleasurable condition in your life. Why? Because gratitude is a lifeline to a broader outlook, an appreciative disposition, and a gracious way of living. We do feel grateful when we meet the person of our dreams and claim the object of our affection. Unfortunately, however, we often take the person and the condition for granted. We often fail to give much thought to the value they add to our life and how they contribute to our daily experiences of happiness and well-being. Gratitude is often a casualty of our feeling that we seldom have enough. No matter how much we have, the object of our affection and the conditions for our happiness lie somewhere in the future. I decided to write this book to demonstrate how gratitude can be a "right now" organizing principle and force in people's lives.

I have used story as the centerpiece for this book. We all stand inside a story. We invite others to stand inside our story and welcome the opportunity to stand inside theirs. Our stories unlock the doors of our hearts and make us welcome guests of one another. They form us into communities and knit us in a web of relationships. They help us appreciate how we are joined in our hopes and how we walk toward similar destinations.

The kitchen table is the site where most stories reappear on holidays and other special occasions. This setting provides a hospitable and safe place for gathering and reminding ourselves of the ways we are invested in one another. The tribal ritual begins when we page through our stories to reminisce about the past and talk about the present. Stories become the grist for conversation and often highlight life-altering transformations in thinking, believing, and acting.

Our stories reveal particulars about where we have been, what we have done, and who we have become. They reintroduce us to the cast of characters and the roles they played. We raise the curtain, the characters take their places, and the drama unfolds. We serve as the director until someone else says, "That reminds me of the time," and they set out to tell part of their story. Each story draws us in to imagine a situation all over again, to place ourselves in the middle of the experience and rediscover the lesson we learned from this encounter with life. Stories are the stable center for our lives and, when told, strengthen the bonds that hold us together.

We use our experiences to write the script for our story. The narrative gradually reveals answers to "meaning of life" questions, which in turn, become the core values we embrace, the beliefs we extol, and the choices we make. The answers provide an internal dialogue that directs our conversations with others. We become part of shared imagination, shared adventures, and a collective memory we draw upon to share our stories. Every story, yours and mine, has the potential for teaching us something beneficial about gratitude. Gratitude is both an object and condition to cherish and to be given away.

I have used my own story as a way to help you own and appreciate your story, to see its potential for making more sense of your life, and to help you decide what really matters to you. I believe telling my story can help you reflect upon your life and rediscover the people who have been instrumental in making your story interesting and worth telling. I also believe my stories will stir your imagination and heighten your interest in the stories you already tell. You will be able to draw from each story something important about who you are, how you became that person, and what your life has to say to others.

I hope you find my stories interesting because of their similarities to your stories. By similarities, I do not necessarily refer to events, but to similar situations, that is, your part in an event, how you fit into it. You may have never watched cows graze in a field, but you know what it is like to be situated in a place where you are soothed by the calm and experience a simple and unexplainable inner peace. You may not have had a close encounter with death, but you know what it is like to be afraid and to be rescued from fear.

And you may not have visited a place where you wanted to be alone and have been deprived of this encounter with the sacred, but you know what it is like to treasure a moment only to be interrupted by something unavoidable. The events may be dissimilar, but the situation helps us find the common denominator that binds us. This book honors gratitude as the common denominator that elevates us as human beings, animates our relationships with each other, and is the durable feature of living faith-filled and fruitful lives.

My story, like yours, is a narrative that only I could have written. My goal has been to rediscover the meaning and significance of various people and events in my life. Each story is the springboard for writing about gratitude, pinpointing its spellbinding qualities, revealing its significance in a well-lived life, and directing readers into ways to find, mine, and use gratitude to enhance and empower the lives of others. Tucked away in every story is something that tells us life is good and to be appreciated. Even in the dark days of hardship and tests of will, we can find shards of gratitude. They remind us of life's many blessings, even in the midst of trials and tribulations.

Together, the stories reveal the elements of a common and unifying sacred purpose — a hopeful account about life simultaneously looking inward and outward. They include trace amounts of everything that makes life difficult and demanding, engrossing and entertaining, happy and wholesome, and meaningful beyond the telling. I have found story to be a refreshingly reflective and richly abundant resource for revealing gratitude.

I invite you to join me in making gratitude a plotline for your life and a plumb line for your hopes.

Introduction

When a small child unwraps a Christmas present from Grandma and Grandpa, his face and manner mirror his disappointment at finding a shirt and trousers. His embarrassed parents intercede, "What do you say to Grandma and Grandpa?" The child offers a compliant and unenthusiastic, "Thank you." He is being taught good manners; he is not being taught gratitude. Gratitude, among other things, is a genuine experience of pleasure that occurs when we come to acknowledge and appreciate our good fortune. It is coming to a realization that life itself is a gift and the fruits of our labor are the reward for prudent choices, imagination and inspiration, and purposeful actions. Thus, before you begin reading about the evolution and results of gratitude in my stories, I want to make a case for gratitude itself.

At the outset, I believe searching for the veins of gratitude that run through the surface and deep regions of our lives is worth the effort. Gratitude is an ideal that serves as a good reason to live, to celebrate what has been given, and what has been received. Gratitude helps us take pleasure in recalling what has been taken for granted and aimlessly deposited along the pathways of life. We only need to look over our shoulder to see how gratitude has been overlooked and underappreciated.

Renewing our acquaintance with gratitude can also restore a relationship vital to our happiness as we awaken to the joy just ahead of us. Using gratitude, we can view life through a lens of abundance rather than scarcity. Gratitude gives us a solid reason to be optimistic about life and stirs the dreams on which hope is built. Gratitude is never without an audience because people thrive on the bread and butter of its affirmations.

Gratitude can create a purposeful design for living, a blueprint for building relationships that become lifelines for living. It is a reason to look beyond oneself. Gratitude in others is the current that connects an outlet and an object. It is a noble effort to see the bright things in life without being unduly influenced by unbridled optimism and idealistic illusions.

Gratitude is waking up each day, looking to the heavens from which all good things have their beginnings, sliding out of bed onto the solid reality of another day, and grasping still another opportunity begging to be taken. The day is a *thank you* yet to be known, born out of imagination and ambition held close to our heart's desire. What better way to invest in a day than to look through the prism of goodness and let the light of our lives cast its spell as a rainbow across the path of others? Gratitude becomes a touchstone for taking one day at a time and refuses to release each day until there is something it can claim as life-giving and life-defining.

Though not a solution to life's problems, gratitude can provide a perspective that changes the way a problem looks and feels. It helps us see with greater clarity rather than letting self-pity cloud the issue or divert our attention from what really matters. We are less likely to make a mountain out of a molehill; we are less tense about the problem and less intense about seeking a solution. We stand humbly before the challenge, yet are determined to deal with it as a dilemma rather than a dead end. We are saved from apologizing for our shameful preoccupation with ourselves. Gratitude has a way of helping shape our lives. With this approach to life, our actions are most often beyond reproach.

When we give ourselves over to gratitude, we are devoting ourselves to doing the right thing and living the right way. We begin each day believing our lives are bountiful and want others to be similarly disposed to life. This belief comes from appreciating the ordinary, refusing to subject life to comparisons, and believing others are doing the best they can under the circumstances. Gratitude flourishes when we are reasonably content with our efforts to become who we can be rather than equating happiness with getting everything we want. A grateful disposition allows us to become useful companions and champions for those who aspire to share our good fortune.

Every good story has its beginning and being in gratitude that in some way permeates and elevates its meaning and memorability. Although a story may stand on its own, gratitude woven into its fabric enriches the design and provides a lesson for living. Gratitude has a stabilizing and solidifying influence on life.

The stories in this book are a jumping-off point for the reader. Each title provides the context for discovery, for exploring the distinctive characteristics of gratitude and their contributions to life-defining attitudes, values, and practices. Each reader's conclusions will no doubt extend beyond the nature, purposes, and benefits of gratitude that I have described. This is as it should be, for each person brings the template of his/her own stories to this experience of storytelling and story experiencing.

As you read my stories, I hope you will read between the lines and think about the times life has delivered something serendipitous and unimaginable to you. You were there to take hold of it and make it your own. Use my words as a springboard for diving into your own. Wrap your feelings around some of mine. Snuggle into the warm places and savor the times you have embraced something special. Use gratitude as a lens for looking at life, as a way to listen to and choreograph your life. Make gratitude a tasteful way to say *thank you* without any conditions attached. Let gratitude touch those places that hurt and heal what ails you.

Reflection activities are included at the end of each chapter. They will help you examine your stories through the prism of gratitude. By doing so, you will be able to:

- Escape from life long enough to let solitude and reflection become twin towers for growth;

- Sift through concrete events to apprehend the life-changing effects of retelling and reliving your story;

- Reflect upon the people and experiences that tell you who you are and to whom you belong;

- Rediscover turning points, critical junctures, and vital intersections that have influenced you; and

- Contemplate and solidify the beliefs and values you profess and honor.

You will find, tucked away in every story, something that tells you life is good and to be appreciated. Even during the dark and dismal days, pinpoints of gratitude illuminate our blessings and fuel our hopes. Telling and reliving our stories helps reveal a deeper conviction in the life paths we've chosen and faith in where we have been. In recalling the particulars of our story, we recognize parts of ourselves we missed or were mistaken about the first time around. We become more ourselves with a renewed sense of meaning and a firmly held purpose.

In summary, I stand upon the conviction that gratitude is the inspiration, the mediator, and animator of all other virtues. It is our most powerful ally in our quest for meaning, purpose, and happiness. It is the best possible antidote when life seems pointless, we seem useless, and the quest for happiness eludes us. Gratitude is also endowed with elements of moral excellence and moral strength. Gratitude, like grace, is a silent partner in our desire to know and be known. It is a blessing that pleases the giver and the receiver. Gratitude never tires of being a favor we give to ourselves and offer to others. It is a stronghold against the uncertainty and unpredictability that can be endless assaults on our sure sense of self.

Gratitude fortifies our humanity and becomes a sign of our having attained the healthy outlook we esteem and prize. Gratitude is not a perfect celebration of life or a panacea for our unhappiness, but it does offer us an outlook that sees behind, before, and ahead of us. And it steps out with confidence and courage because it is rooted in faith, hope, and love.

CHAPTER 1

Acceptance

*Gratitude accepts without
prior expectations.*

In childhood we collect memories, rarely thinking about them at the time. Rather, we busily make ourselves and our world. Each day's activities seem like a set of wooden building blocks. The letters and colors on the blocks provide a multitude of combinations. We arrange and rearrange them according to the *moment's pleasure*. Life doesn't have to be taken too seriously because we have plenty of time to stack and unstack our experiences, stretch them out, build them up, and even topple our structures and start all over again.

What playfully goes up and comes down is mirrored in our interior life. Our daily activities reveal structures that serve as reference points relating us to the world and to important people in it. They remind us of where we have been and what we have done. They become the stories we tell "about the times when."

During my childhood I spent a week every summer with my grandparents in Litchville, North Dakota, population 500. The highlight was helping my grandfather deliver milk he bottled twice a day from his small dairy herd. Before each day's milk deliveries, milk from the herd was poured from pails into large metal containers in the barn. The milk cans, each of which held several gallons, were carried to a separate milk house near the barn to be cooled. Then the contents were poured into a huge metal bowl at the top of a device to separate the cream from the milk. The milk was transferred to glass bottles placed on a metal stand below the bowl. Then my grandfather capped each bottle with a cardboard bottle cap using a device similar to a pump handle. With this device, he secured a cap complete with pull-tab, inside the ring around the bottle's neck. The bottles were then placed in a cooler of cold water.

My grandfather's position as the "town's milkman" defined his life from one day to the next. Because he was never in a hurry, it didn't bother him when I tagged along. He lived one day at a time, content with what each day offered. In 1940 I was six years old and had a similar outlook on life. Activities of *tomorrow* did not compete for our attention while today's activities still offered pleasure and happiness.

The distance between my grandparents' house, pasture, barn, and a dozen square blocks of Litchville's worn-dirt roads defined the geography of my grandfather's job. This was a small world with simple expectations. It promised a comfortable, reassuring contrast to the endless, and seldom traversed, neighborhoods of St. Louis, Missouri, where I lived at the time. In Litchville I could wander far and wide and still never be very far from where I needed to be when it was time for milking and milk delivery. I felt like the barn cats that rested contentedly in the hayloft overnight. They always knew when it was time for breakfast and supper. They waited until they heard the ping of a stream of milk hitting the bottom of the tin milking pail. Then they would scamper down the ladder from hayloft to milking floor, scurrying to locate my grandfather in anticipation of a treat. He would turn a cow's teat in their direction, stroke the teat, and send a stream of liquid refreshment in their direction. The cats lunged toward the stream that splattered across their faces, licked themselves clean, and waited for my grandfather to send another stream of milk their way. The cats followed my grandfather and his bucket as he made his way down the stanchions, addressing each cow by name, and adding appreciative remarks. Replete, the cats would wander off and disappear in the barnyard until the next milking time.

I generally participated in the late afternoon milking and second delivery of the day. Over the years my grandfather gradually gave me more adult-like opportunities to show my mettle as a city boy learning how to be a farmer and a man.

Gratitude blossoms in the right place at the right time.

In my farm education, my first stunning thrill came when my grandfather gave me a chance to call the cows in from their grazing pasture across the road from the farm. To alert the cows to start for the barn, my grandfather shouted shrilly to attract their attention. The lead cow, Betsy, raised up, looked in his direction, stood momentarily to check him out, and then made her way to the pasture gate. The large copper bell around her neck clanged as it swayed side to side in sync with her gait. Like the Pied Piper, the lingering sound seemed to create a path behind her where the herd followed.

Images of Betsy also conjure up my memories of lazy afternoons lying in a hammock beneath a dense stand of oak trees with sunlight dancing through the shadows. I listened to Betsy's bell as she made her way around the pasture, periodically stopping to satisfy her hunger. The sound changed as the clapper danced about inside the bell. I could tell where Betsy was and what she was doing by listening to the pitch, clarity, and cadence of the instrument around her neck. The sound drifting slowly across the landscape mirrored the pace of the day. I was comforted by these small assurances that separated one day from the next when life did not demand much, nor was much expected of it.

Gratitude rests comfortably where it is.

Our efforts to fill every moment of the day with productivity and accomplishment disturb and undermine the natural rhythm of life. We leave no time to settle down and rest with the in-between times. Rest, unlike work, doesn't produce anything tangible. Although it feels good, there is nothing to show for an expenditure of time. Thus, we find it difficult to justify naps, meditation, or mid-day walks; we wonder what we could have done if we hadn't engaged in such frivolous activities. Unlike cats, we resist curling up and taking leave of everything else. We envy their contentment, but we just can't rest until everything else is done.

Expectations create our daily agenda; we can never be sure we have done enough. Leftover tasks are packed up and lifted onto the shoulder of another today. In our breathless rush to catch up, we cannot accept and celebrate the fruits of one day's labor. Instead we are simultaneously drawn in all directions; life becomes a hassle and a blur.

Thus, today we talk about multitasking. We pride ourselves on carrying on a simultaneous conversation with past, present, and future. It is not enough to accept and honor each task with our full attention and respectful efforts. Instead, a full life appears packed to the brim. Leftover tasks spill over and leave no time dividing one task from another. Everything is about *adding tasks* and *multiplying productivity*. Bent on maximizing our technological capabilities, we whir along at breakneck speed. We cannot keep up, so we are dragged along into the fast lane. There we race against ourselves, making life a competition. *We have to beat up on ourselves to win!*

Gratitude's staying power has a punch.

This was not the pace in my grandfather's barn. Entering those four walls was crossing over into a different time *dimension*. Life was simpler and predictably saner. Admittedly, the simplicity may color my current judgment; the predictability may provide a safe haven from reality. Time may cleanse our memories of hardship and the mundane. It can also distance us from truth and give us the freedom to create our own comforting memories. By exaggerating past over present, we imagine much more than what was then and much less of what is now. Such selective memory is generally rooted in sentiment and is long on feelings we can lovingly embrace. Tampering with the past may lack objectivity, but it reintroduces us to ourselves and provides a hospitable way to become a guest of our hearts.

Whether past or present, life is perpetually prompting us to ask, "Who am I?" Delivering bottles of milk with my grandfather helped define me. I cannot, and would not, exchange that experience for something else or try to find its equivalent today. Its lasting effects may not be easily discernible, but the decision to write about the experience attests to its enduring meaning. Such slivers and slices of life prompt our thoughts, lie lightly on our hearts, and press us into honoring our past and building our future. We accept something of how we were treated and regarded. Acceptance is a pearl of great price raised from the soil of approving affirmations and celebratory events.

Gratitude trusts the present and the future.

Grandpa delivered milk twice daily, before dawn and just before dusk. He used a horse and wagon equipped with a large, four-sided wooden box with doors hinged at the top on each side. Inside, slotted boards divided the box to accommodate various-sized bottles and keep them from tilting or sliding. Still, the wooden wagon wheels did not provide a cushioned ride and *the sound of bottles clanking* was exaggerated by the quiet around us as we made our rounds.

The open-air wagon cab had no seat belts or doors to protect us from falling out. We sat high above the horse, perched on a wooden bench-like structure with a fashionably styled black leather seatback. Our single-horse powered engine pulled the load forward effortlessly, responding to a pair of reins and a gentle voice. No sparkplugs or battery required. The gas tank consisted of oats and an occasional apple for this simple, reliable conveyance. We would never exceed a speed limit or go much faster than the pace Joe, grandfather's horse, set for himself. And what did it matter? We didn't have far to go and seldom was anyone waiting for us to get there.

Gratitude weaves itself into lifelong memories.

Joe was no ordinary means of transportation, even in 1940. Once under way, he did not need a satellite guidance system. He was a man about town and knew the delivery route. Without benefit of brakes, Joe slowed and stopped as he approached the first destination. My grandfather knew each family's regular order and told me what to take. If there were any order changes, we found a note on the dairy box outside each door.

At each stop my grandfather and I clambered down from opposite sides of our perch, each with a metal milk carrier that held six bottles of milk. We opened a side door on the wooden box and grasped the pronounced ring around each bottle's neck. I can still feel the smooth surface as each bottle slipped through my hands into the carrier, milk in quart bottles and cream in stubby pint ones. A carrier with six bottles of milk was a manly load for me. But no one suggested it might be too heavy or that this was a grand achievement. Rather, I received an unspoken acceptance that saved me from being overly dependent on the opinion of others later in life.

As soon as we started our trip to the house, Joe began a slow gait to the next stop. If we needed additional milk at a stop, my grandfather quietly addressed Joe with a "whoa." In these rare instances Joe pulled up without hesitation and remained still until we supplied a customer's request. I marveled at Joe's effortless, *error-free,* and dutiful stop-and-go performance. When we climbed back onto the wagon, Joe knowingly waited for my grandfather to record each household's purchases in his ledger.

This accounting system was as uncomplicated and straightforward as life itself at that time. After the sale was duly entered and a gentle shake of the reins, Joe accelerated to about five miles an hour. The orderliness I saw in all of these transactions left a permanent imprint and preference for organization on my personality. There is something magical about everything having a place and being in its place.

Gratitude waits without an agenda.

More human relationships should be patterned after the bond I observed between a man and another of God's creatures. Even at my tender age, the respect and loyalty between my grandfather and Joe were not lost on me. An endearing quality joined man and beast, although Joe was more like a pet. A bucket of oats and a bucket of water stored under the cab seat were occasionally offered to show affection and affirmation, not as an incentive. Joe probably would have pulled that wagon and us the entire morning and evening without expecting anything. An unconditional bond formed between these two parties — the person on the wagon and the horse drawing it forward.

This milking and delivery enterprise totally engaged me. In one sense my grandfather and I were business partners, but I also saw us as companions on a journey. The deliveries seemed a way of getting to know and appreciate each other. Over the course of our deliveries, my grandfather cast out lines of unspoken reciprocity. They connected us to something special and remind me today of two men doing a job and drawing something out of each other in the doing. It wasn't what was said but what was felt as two generations found a common place to meet and exchange the intrinsic value of respect. We started in different places, took different pathways and still, by chance and circumstance, met at a crossroads and continued on together. Acceptance built bridges between our disparate experiences and our separate longings. What we discovered in each other forever bound us, and we gladly claimed the effects.

I felt grateful to simply be part of this adventure with Joe and my grandfather. Yet, at the end of each delivery as we prepared for the next day, my grandfather reached into his pocket and asked me to open my hands. He counted out and poured five Indian head pennies into the gulf of my outstretched hands. Always five. They seemed to come from an endless supply, a mystery I never questioned. This exchange was a sacred moment. Nothing could make it any better.

Gratitude offers a timeless supply of being enough.

I never spent any of those delivery pennies. For years I deposited my summer treasures in a fruit jar. They represented hard cash with modest economic value, circular tokens that rounded out a period of time in my life. During World War II, with a shortage of copper for the war effort, I exchanged my "history pennies" for history in the making and purchased a $25 war savings bond. As my dad and uncles were serving our country, it felt like I purchased a little patriotism with those pennies.

I no longer need those objects to revisit the memories or to revitalize the spirit of the original offering. But as a young boy I lacked the mental tools I have today to resurrect and reconstruct the way life was then and make something new of it. That is the beauty of our memories. They secure us to the past and become our mainstays in

reliving and reinterpreting the past. I can rediscover relationships and the context and the content that reconnect me
with what was meant to be more than I originally thought
it could be. However old we are, reaching back is only an
arm's length away to how our hearts felt at the time.

Gratitude announces itself without fanfare.

The story of milk deliveries illustrates how a one-on-
one relationship changed with the maturing of one party
and the thoughtful recognition of changes in the other. We
have all been children gradually drawn into the adult world
when someone sees something in us and draws it out with a
pioneering spirit of adventure. Faith in someone else is the
common ground that leaves an indelible imprint on each
other's mind and heart. Gratitude, with its lasting power,
helps us hold onto the faith of the moment.

You may not have had an experience like mine, but
counterpoints in some experience undoubtedly speak to you
in a similar voice and leave traces of the experience using
a similar language. The event itself is less important than
what you brought to it and what you took away from it.
Looking upon my life with gratitude helps me reinvent and
reinvest myself in something that matters. Death cannot
separate me from my grandfather nor can time erase the
experiences that bound us. Gratitude becomes an enduring
reminder and seals a permanent bond.

REFLECTION TODAY

Think of a person who took you into his or her life and let you be who you were then. You were disposed to accept what was offered and given without the pressure of expectations or evaluations. When you recall this relationship, think of a specific way you spent time together with this other person. Now dwell on the features of the experience that made the relationship natural without wanting or needing anything more.

REFLECTION TOMORROW

Select one of the most meaningful and joyful moments disclosed in yesterday's reflection. Retrieve a specific behavior — something said or done — like my grandfather pouring five Indian head pennies into my hand or my experience sitting next to him in the wagon as business partners making our rounds. Use this tangible behavior as a springboard to think about something you can say to or do for someone to give that person a lift through your gratitude.

CHAPTER 2

Hardship

Gratitude bears hardship
without complaint.

We often learn the most enduring and far-reaching lessons of gratitude from what life has chosen for us and forced upon us. Every story told revives an experience and rediscovers the storyteller's perspective. Sometimes two people can share parts of a similar story, yet what looms large in their minds is vastly different. Often differences are due to selective recall of the event itself, where each person was at that time in his or her life, how an event became a growing experience of living, or what part each person played to create the story itself.

My father and I both had a dairy story. Mine took place during summers between 1940-1942 when I helped with my grandfather's milk delivery route. My father's took place during winter in the 1920s. He was not casually involved in making his story as I was, nor as kindly treated by circumstances surrounding his story. His conclusions about the good old days, at least in this instance, do not correspond to my own.

Unquestionably, my father and I came at our recollections of the cows in our dairy stories based on *entirely* different circumstances. His recollections are much more emotionally charged by work and hardship experiences. My story is couched in pleasurable and leisurely excursions. Mine left me feeling privileged and undamaged by the trials and tribulations of North Dakota's hard winters. His story is recorded in the recesses of his mind and comes tumbling out at the mere mention of winter and cows. My story is encased in my heart and cascades out like a flowing stream when the floodgate of memories is opened.

Gratitude enables us to live with uncertainty.

Like all of us, my father did not choose part of his story. He lived on a small acreage on the edge of Litchville, North Dakota, population 500. He was eleven years old when his father died. To support her family of five, his mother started a dairy. She sold the family's two horses and bought two cows and a cream separator. Two years later she came up with an idea that eliminated all competition: "Free delivery of milk to your home twice a day." Delivering the milk through the seasons of the year was not nearly as difficult as caring for the two — soon to be four — cows, particularly given the increase in the amount of water they could consume during the winter. During the spring, summer, and fall, the cows drank out of the town's artesian spring-fed water tank. Even during part of winter the cows could be taken out of the barn and driven downtown to drink. Because the tank was fed with a continuous stream of water, the amount they drank did not matter. They drank until they were satisfied. But after a North Dakota blizzard deposited huge and uneven banks of snow, the cows could not go to the water — the water had to be taken to them! Then the amount they drank was brought forcibly to the attention of my father and his older brother.

I relished hearing my father and uncle tell, often at my urging, about how the cows' thirst multiplied many times over during the worst of winter's awful days. This part of their story is rooted in a disputable claim that is arguably credible when examined from my father's point of view. My father claimed, contrary to what one might expect, dairy cows were thirstier in the winter than in the summer. In fact, he contended, you could predict their thirst by the severity of the blizzard and the arctic temperature outside. Although not a statistician, he asserted that there was a direct and perfect correlation between these two conditions. Statisticians generally work with variables that do not match this perfect level of significance. But Dad insisted that when temperatures fell, there was a corresponding *increase* of amount of falling, blinding snow blowing across the open area between the town well and the barn. As these two cruel conditions grew worse, so too, did the thirst of the cows. There was a striking predictability between the harshness of the weather and demand for satisfaction by the cows. The two measures were also predictable from one trip to the town's water tank to the next, just as one day follows the next. Despite only being a mile, this distance, according to my father's story, would severely test the stamina and endurance of a marathon runner. Just as the runner dare not become dehydrated, the cows demanded to be replenished to stay the course.

Gratitude favors circumstances that point in the same direction.

Once aroused by this part of their story, my father and uncle did not have to be implored to continue. They would cast the trip to town in the aftermath of a story. I can readily recall my father's description of a North Dakota blizzard. The flat, wide-open space offered no resistance to the fury of the wind, creating chaos with huge amounts of falling snow. A rope was the only secure way to get from house to barn. Immediately upon opening the door from the house, one would take hold of the rope and cling to it, hand-over-hand, using it as a security line. The snow was so dense and blinding, one could not see the barn until it was well within reach. He also claimed — and his brother said it was no exaggeration — in the middle of a storm you could not see your hand when placed directly in front of your face. In many instances, people who misjudged the force of the wind and snow and wandered out into a borderless world were not found until the snow melted in the spring.

Litchville was a forlorn, desolate place after a storm and its citizens did not venture out. There was no commercial activity along the three-block trek down Main Street. The town water tank, generally a hub of activity, was deserted. Two young boys, somewhat daunted by these conditions and beckoned by necessity, had to leave behind warmth and security to haul water for the cows. Despite their small frames, they had to do the work of two sturdy and hardened men. Head-strong, valiant, and resolute, they set out from home pulling a home-made conveyance — a wooden sled with a large, empty barrel atop — to haul water to the herd. The boys checked to make sure the barrel was firmly roped to the sled. Loneliness filled the space between each breath of frigid, moist air during their trek.

Small clouds gathered between each puff. They could only imagine what was going on behind closed doors and windows draped with blankets. This was the first vital step in what would be a test of wills and strength.

Across this barren and wide expanse of snow-laden ground, the boys would make their way to the town water tank to fill the barrel. The trip from home was generally not a problem. Difficulty began when they scooped water with a pail from the water trough and poured it into the barrel. They had to exercise some care not to spill water down the sides of the barrel, adding to its weight and slipperiness. The elements did not conspire until my father and his older brother were returning with a full barrel of water balanced precariously on the sled. Buildings along the main street snuggled against one another and provided some shield against the elements. The road surface was reasonably smooth, unaffected by wind and drifting snow. Yet there were some frozen bobsled tracks and lumps of hard snow, so the going was not entirely smooth.

However, when they began to trudge into the wind along the path toward the barn, the conditions shifted ominously. Their wavering bodies, combined with the uneven surface beneath the sled, conspired against them. As the sled leaned from side to side, the water sloshed about in the barrel, disturbing the even distribution of fluid. The water began to splash out and to freeze down the sides of the barrel and onto the sled. Although they could have reduced this disastrous spillage by putting less water in the barrel, the boys wanted to minimize the number of trips. Two conditions conflicted with one another: the aggregate of various emotions and the volume of water the barrel could contain. Temperate minds would have come down on the side of reason to travel with less water in the barrel. However, logic was overridden in their desire to reduce the number of trips. The brothers placed their bets on having honed some barrel- and sled-steadying skills. It was a big gamble, but they were driven to take a chance. They risked keeping the barrel upright as one pulled the sled and the other steadied the shifting and treasured contents.

Gratitude reminds us life is seldom as bad as it seems.

The sled would become a problem when they reached an open area of about 100 yards between the house and the barn, an area without trees to lessen the impact of the wind or prevent drifting of a heavy snowfall. Here, so close to accomplishing their mission, they would have to traverse the steep sides of a *densely* packed snowdrift in the open space between the house and barn. Invariably, as my dad told the story, when he reached this point, he was already weary from keeping the barrel upright. The sides were ice covered, and it perched precariously on a slippery surface. Dad's mittens were covered with ice and his hands were numb. All conditions worked against these two boys winning their bet against the hazardous elements facing them. Two small, vulnerable boys, a sled with a slick surface, and an ice-covered barrel were no match for drifts four to five feet high. *Their gamble rarely paid out.*

Water would slop out and cascade down the barrel's side and fall onto a snowdrift already packed down by the relentless pounding of the wind. The water would run across the drift's icy surface. The barrel leaned like grass on a wind-swept prairie; sled runners found no foothold to resist impending disaster. Yet they had to go forward. The older brother would give last-minute instructions and reassuring comments about being strong and tough. As one pulled the rope attached to the sled, the other would push while being splattered by water splashing down the sides of the barrel. Often efforts to keep the barrel upright were futile because of the bank's slope. The pressure of so much weight on one runner would lift the other runner from the surface. The entire sequence of events would go so quickly there was nothing to do but fall away from the tragedy unfolding. Physics would not yield its principles despite heroic efforts of two struggling boys. The contents of the barrel spilled over the sled, the snow bank, the boys, and their dampened spirits. They had to start all over. But their next trip would be even more hazardous because they would be going both directions with an ice-laden sled and barrel.

In his later years my dad compared their battle with the elements to a military campaign in World War II. Their warfare was against an enemy intent upon binding them to the dictates of a totalitarian regime! They enlisted for the duration and engaged the enemy regardless of the hardships, setbacks, and retreats. They only took temporary leave of the fray and their duties to make themselves battle ready again, this time more determined, stronger, and wiser. Well, at least determined. Willpower served as their shield, pride as their weapons, and resilience as their honor. Courage and boldness were their coat of arms.

My dad's telling included descriptions of bitter cold that seemed to penetrate and do battle with every bone in his body. Even soldiers cry when a fierce battle takes its toll. When this happened, tears were a balm that soothed his weary body and calmed his broken heart. Sitting by the heat of a wood-burning stove had its salutary effects, and he was also warmed by his mother's comforting arms and consoling words. However, sometimes between sobs, he would protest and insist he was not going out again. Just the thought of returning for another load, with no assurance the water would not spill again, was too much for him. Yet his brother, two years older, stronger, and with an indomitable spirit urged him to toughen up and be resolute. His brother was a battle-worn and disciplined leader who knew much depended upon his commission to uphold their honor and lead the next charge. My dad was still laboring against horrendous odds, not schooled enough to imagine victory nor mature enough to imagine something to celebrate.

Yet the boys could not turn away from duty. They had no choice but to go back and engage the enemy in yet another battle to bring water to quench the cows' thirst. The cows were their livelihood, their freedom from want, and their hope for the future. Their countrymen expected no less than what they were doing to battle the elements and arrive at the barn door having declared a victory over the enemy.

Gratitude's loving intentions strengthen our willpower.

My dad claims they never warmed up before they had to fight against the elements again. Just knowing this was enough to send shivers down his brutally sensitized body. He knew full well the return try to get water would be an even more delicate balancing act and with a potentially disheartening outcome. This time they were dealing with an ice-covered snow bank that took on mountainous proportions looming but a short distance from their destination.

Dad's shoulders already ached from the first assault. He was bent over by the thought of what was yet to come. His body was not immune to dreadful emotions. Together they formed an obstacle between what he needed to do and his reason for doing it. He could not permit himself to be confused. As the boys approached the ice-covered drift the second time, they would stop and assess the situation like civil engineers. They surveyed the area to see if they could lessen their vulnerability and make the best of the situation. Then they charted their course. At times, they chose a detour that increased the distance but avoided the obvious hazards. They learned a straight line is not always the shortest distance between two points. At the end of the journey, sometimes they succeeded. Other times they repeated the dreadful routine of changing clothes, trying to get warm, relieving themselves of anger and despair, and psychologically preparing themselves to try again.

Sometimes when they braved the elements, they seized the day and won a small victory: They made it to the barn door. There they would use a pail to dip water out of the barrel and take a proportionate amount to each cow until the barrel was empty. The boys held the pail of water up to each cow's mouth while she drank. When the cows had finished the last of the two or three pails full, my dad claimed they would look sorrowfully at him and my uncle as if to say, "Surely there is more where this came from." While they felt sorry for the cows, they thought it would be so nice to quit and go into the house to stay. However, it was difficult to resist the disquieting effects of mournful eyes and a low pleading moo for more. Invariably they would rest from their labor and the older brother would decide. They would return to the town for another load.

Gratitude bends the laws of human nature.

It may be difficult to discover any gratitude when we encounter devastating assaults on our certitude and are tested by the inherent limitations of body and spirit. Yet a sense of accomplishment and thankfulness arises when we are able to derail the effects of adversity and surmount our tendency to shortchange ourselves when the going gets tough. Gratitude emerges from the relief of having done what had to be done and doing it in spite of our doubts and a few glimmers of hope. My dad felt fleeting gratitude for the warmth and comfort between repeated trips on a given day. Gratitude may come in small doses, but each offer can produce some healing effects. Every adversity has its limits and cannot endlessly perpetuate itself.

Gratitude buttresses patience and persistence.

My dad survived the desolate days of winter and water-carrying adversity. But desolation can be devastating when it takes up residence inside of us. Yet what seems like an eternity in one's mind has a hope-enduring counterpart in one's heart. We also have a balance-striving scale in our souls. God's finger rests ever so slightly on one edge. We can be optimistic and hopeful because the rim will always be tilted toward a love that endures all things.

Love was the spindle and hope the wool that my grandmother used to knit a blanket to wrap two young boys into a lifelong devotion to one another. I felt and observed this fraternal relationship when I asked them to retell the dairy cow story. As I recount this event, I re-engage myself in the spirit of devotion that held them together and endured a lifetime. We all long to hear and participate in stories that offer us life-giving strands connecting us to the deeper meaning of our existence. Sacrifice is a strand-bearing experience we knit into long-lasting relationships. We tie off the ends when the weaving has been completed. Between one end and the other are stirring and sterling lessons of friendship and fidelity. Each lesson may include recognition of something special and soul binding about the relationship.

As an unmarried teacher/coach, my uncle spent Christmas vacations with us and visited us over many years. When I asked to hear the dairy cow story told again and again, I could detect the special bond of fondness and fidelity that endeared my father and uncle to one another. The years did not alter the story facts, but the retelling did transport us into new revelations of caring. The retelling became not just about the hardships but also about tenacity and endurance in the face of relentless challenges. The brothers shared the satisfaction of saving their childhood while learning how to provide for the family's livelihood. They even showed an undertow of affection in their remarks about the cows. These boys stood together against adversity with a widowed mother who also stood up against it, molding two boys into men and members of a family that included a herd of dairy cows.

Gratitude's resilience puts endurance to the test.

I am grateful I know this story ... the facts of it and what the story reveals in spaces between the facts. Joy is stepping into these spaces and residing there long enough to merge the spirit and facts into revelations of our sacred connections to one another. We are introduced to gratitude as we are included in a heart-wrenching, heartwarming experience of the indomitable spirit of frontier people and in my case a heritage of stubbornly independent, relentless, and richly blessed ancestors. My dad and uncle taught me that some things in life demand a staunch heart and a resolute belief in oneself. The conviction is forged from being able to surmount any difficulty and refusing to be worn down to the core of one's disbelief. Gratitude reminds us of our tenacity and creates a dauntless rediscovery of being rescued from those difficult years.

Gratitude travels the distance beyond hardship.

Sometimes gratitude is only an afterthought. We don't make much of it. We are content with the temporary tutelage it offers us. At other times we grasp its power and cling to its nobility. Sometimes gratitude launches us into a realm where life meets a simple reality. We wave off its significance. Sometimes gratitude becomes a resource for making life better long after the meaning inspired by events has drifted beyond our grasp. But particles of gratitude's splendor continue to sparkle amid the dailiness of our lives. Others see the glow and feel the warmth. We are first-hand witnesses and second-hand advocates for gratitude.

At other times, we may come along as interlopers long after others have found much to be grateful about. We sometimes find ourselves so full of self-pity and self-consternation that gratitude cannot find a place to reside, much less an opportunity to be lived. Thankfulness sometimes feels like a past we cannot remember and a future that is a bleak reminder that little good will come from this one. Yet, being freed from a dreadful situation can give one pause to be grateful. Being shown a bright spot in the road can be an incentive to go on. We can draw upon the power of comparisons to see our hardships pale when held up against the plight of many others. Perspective can help us realize gratitude can be a gift that keeps giving. As we have been released, at least temporarily, from hardship, we can now surrender part of our time and self to be available to someone in need. Gratitude can be put in the service of small acts of kindness and can serve to revive an earlier day of limitless promise.

Gratitude's promise is always on our radar screen.

Gratitude can put its arms around any hardship, give it a hug, and make it feel better. It is like a mother who caresses a child and offers the simple comfort of a few heart-chosen words: "It will be okay. Mother loves you. I will help make it better." Gratitude doesn't have to search for words. They are conceived and born of life-giving experiences. They linger in the heart as the incarnation of goodness. They spill over and pour out as acts of reassurance when all else seems to fail. We are never lost or far from goodness when gratitude remembers hardship and offers ways to make the most of its possibilities for growth.

We grow into gratitude like any other virtue. Gratitude is not a birthright but becomes one for those who believe life can be better and adopt an adventurous spirit to prove their point. Some are born into hardship and spend their entire life bemoaning it as intrusive. Others use hardship as a test of will and as a challenge to surmount. They develop and rely upon other virtues to take hardship apart, reassemble its pieces, and use them to build a new life. My dad and his brother looked for relief from hardship by becoming a three-ply cord and pulling together. They found strength in fierce loyalty to one another, unfettered determination to succeed, and patient endurance in the face of adversity. They refused to ask "Why?" They accepted the situation and asked what could be done to deal with it. They took appropriate steps to minimize the consequences of defeat. They cut the situation down to a manageable solution and made the most of what they were given. Asking "why" often deflates one's determination and throws up roadblocks to action. They rode on the back of previous successes. Equipped with gratitude for what they had done before, they set out each time believing they would win out against the elements because virtue always triumphs over hardship.

Gratitude whittles down adversity.

Hardship takes bits and pieces of raw experience, combined with repeated acts of efficacy and goodness, and molds them into virtues. We think and believe in the ultimate victory of passion and purpose put into service of noble aspirations. We come into gratitude as we sift through courageous acts of self-giving, seasoned acts of stamina, unwavering faith in self and others, and honorable celebrations of our successes. With well-calibrated hearts, we have been taught by the daily life-bracing experiences of thankfulness and gratitude. Life is not taken for granted. There is always tomorrow. We can look to life's possibilities by drawing upon yesterday's experience of gratitude and its striking power to inform all of life.

REFLECTION TODAY

No one is a stranger to hardship. We generally do not welcome it. Thus it generally enters our lives through the back door. Once inside, we have no choice but to deal with it. What we decide to do can make it a life-giving or death-dealing experience. Hardship is life-giving when we live with it long enough to see what it is all about, what it offers to us, what lessons we can learn to make something good of the experience. Hardship is death-dealing when we hold it at arm's length, refusing to let it come closer to us, dismissing the message, and ignoring the consequences. Between these two states of mind and two approaches to life, we can learn much from hardship and gain much to be thankful for upon its departure.

Recall a hardship, a single incident or an extended period of time, when you found life hardly bearable by circumstances beyond your control. You did not choose the hardship as a form of sacrificial giving or as a way of disciplining yourself to relinquish a bad habit. This hardship brought you into the grips of suffering that would not let go. It refused to give into your efforts to minimize its impact and its effects. As you rediscover the thoughts and feelings, retrace your actions. What did you learn to be grateful about following this difficult encounter with life? How has this gratitude influenced your outlook on life and the way you think of yourself? How has it influenced how you respond to the hardship of others?

REFLECTION TOMORROW

Yesterday you recalled a single and naturally occurring hardship in your life. You selected this hardship as a way of seeing what it did to you, and possibly others, as a life-giving and death-dealing experience.

Hardships do not always just happen to us. Sometimes we choose hardships to help us grow into something or someone we want to be. For example, we may decide to make a change in our lives, possibly to be more grateful for what we have been given and what we have received. This decision may occur when we realize how much we take for granted after seeing others' losses or lack of basic necessities of life.

Or we may choose a hardship because we are not sufficiently happy with appearance, bad personal habits (smoking or drinking to excess), or our ability to deal with hardship itself.

Recall a decision you made to take on a hardship by the nape of the neck, even though you resisted. Choose a hardship in which your determination, patience, and perseverance produced the desired and grateful outcome. What hardship did you decide to bear? Why this particular choice from among many others you might have chosen? What roadblocks, thoughts, feelings, actions, and challenges did you encounter? How did you deal with the obstacles? What do you think accounted for your success? Did your success encourage you to deliberately introduce hardship into your life again, and if so, for what purpose?

CHAPTER 3

Friendship

*Gratitude launches us
into the fullness of life.*

My family moved from a sizable urban city in
Minnesota to Clarion, a small town in Iowa at the outset
of my sophomore year in high school. I could not imagine
a greater personal calamity or a justifiable reason for my
dad to uproot us once again. We had lived in Freeport and
Chicago, Illinois; St. Louis, Missouri; Braham and St.
Cloud (twice), Minnesota; Estherville, Iowa, and now we
moved to Clarion, Iowa. I already knew what it was like to
be torn by uncertainty and dragged into the irregularity of
another life. This was my seventh time being thrown into
the unknown during my fifteen years. It is a terrible feeling to pull up anchor and be set adrift without a compass.
I knew the devastating feelings of loneliness, the painful
departures and unwelcome experiences yet to come, the
frightening experience of being pushed out onto the stage of
life without the benefit of any lines to say. All I could think
about was exchanging the comfortable, stable space in my
life for the empty space into which I was being thrust. It
was unnerving to be separated from one end of life without

knowing anyone at the other end. I could not foresee any thing good coming out of this situation even though I had successfully conquered melancholy and foreboding in the past. I had learned to cope in the interval between being left out and being let in again. I knew I could take up residence somewhere else and eventually be more than a resident or an occupant. There are people everywhere who welcome opportunities to meet someone new and risk the initial awkwardness of the introduction.

Yet, it is not easy to leave one's friends. They were durable and predictable companions who could not be replaced easily like exchangeable parts on an assembly line. They were friends with whom I had shared a thousand pleasures and upbeat experiences. I relied upon them for happy recollections that had become a stable source of anticipations and surprises at the beginning of every day. They were the cast of characters with whom I knew my role and the drama of life unfolding.

Gratitude sees beyond our limited perspectives when all else fails.

I did receive some expected and curious looks during the first week of high school classes. New was the only thing I had to offer, but they were not buying. They were already heavily invested in one another. They were not willing to speculate when they already had a sure thing. And why should they? They had made their friendship choices long before I came on the scene. Time had strengthened those ties. I was merely a novelty.

I brought with me well-established habits of another adolescent culture. A bicycle was a common and dependable means of transportation where I came from. Although it was an oddity in this setting, I did not relinquish the practice. Later I learned that, at least to the football coach, it was an admirable attitude and commendable "workout." My grooming habits and attire also set me apart. I wore what I brought with me: loafers, white socks, and Levi jeans with neatly twice-rolled cuffs. Each of these choices stood in contrast to what other guys were wearing at my new school. The distinction was not lost on the young women and was later adopted by some of their boyfriends. I also brought with me a distinctive Brylcreem look — hair in a swept-back wave born of pride and self-importance. Sometimes differences attract. But change doesn't occur overnight.

Gratitude uses earlier success as a foothold in a new situation.

I looked for the day when my prowess on the football field would change my status, so that I could prove I belonged in this realm of student life. I had played football in junior high. I had been one of three freshmen invited to spring practice at a large public metropolitan high school. This move to Clarion would separate me from being a sophomore on the varsity team that fall. I decided to try to make my way into this new situation by relying on something that had distinguished me in the past. Some things in life cannot easily be overlooked; demonstrated abilities are out there for all to see. I reported for football practice confident I could impress the coaches and shake up the existing order among competitors. I came as a left halfback with proven accomplishments at this position. I knew I would have to demonstrate my *adroitness* to those who had already laid claim to this position. I was a threat to some and a *curiosity* to others. I was daring to challenge the status quo and make an issue where none seemed to exist. I was shaking up their world just as mine had been shaken. The tremors would be more keenly felt once I was tried against the prevailing conclusions about who was in and out.

For most, athletics is an outlet for those willing to test their ability and demonstrate their worth in a clash of will and talent. At the outset, at least, I felt acknowledged, if not accepted. I only wanted to be given a chance to let my speed, skill, and previous success speak for me. Being a player superseded being a friend; I was more interested in making the team than making friends. I knew the first would likely lead to the other. Previous experience verified this conclusion. Time would tell whether it would work again. As it turned out, three guys who would become my best friends played quarterback, right halfback, and left tackle. They chose me. Then I chose them. This had been the irreversible order I had become accustomed to during the previous uprootings. We were practically inseparable throughout our high school years. I have stood next to them, before them, and with them through all the vicissitudes of life. Gratitude continues to remind me that playing a game became the forerunner and mainstay for a lifetime of special alliances and treasured memories.

I vividly remember the breakthrough moment during the first game we played my sophomore year. A senior started at left halfback. He had established himself as the best player at this position. I was but a newcomer and a largely unknown challenger. I did get into the game during the fourth quarter. On the third defensive play the opponent's quarterback underestimated my quickness, and his teammates misjudged my speed. I was fifty-four yards too deceptive. The sideline was a clear path to the end zone. I was no longer someone who had come to be content to stand on the sidelines. This would be the first of many coming-off-the-bench successes. Leaving the bench, I became a participant as a newcomer. A coach can change the cast of characters, rewrite the story line, and the plot. For me achievement on the field became a stepping-stone on the path to friendship.

Gratitude resides at the intersection of uncertainty and hope.

After the game, as I celebrated the winning combination of our defense and my fourth-quarter heroics, I met one of the cheerleaders as she departed from a gathering of her friends. She greeted me by name and extended a few words of congratulations. I can to this day remember my name being spoken as though I was somebody. It was the turning point, from uncertainty to hopefulness, from isolation to acceptance. Practice on the following Monday began a gradual acceptance as a member of the football family. Three guys stepped out of the wings and a lifelong drama began. Others would become members of a cast of characters who made important contributions to my claiming Clarion as my hometown. I suppose, in one sense, it couldn't be any other way because my parents continued to reside there for the remainder of their lives. But a hometown is more than a residence or where mail is delivered. A hometown is the residual effects of all the happenings that make life something to remember and talk about. It is all the conclusions we come to believe about ourselves and people who end up being right in the middle of them. It is about looking ahead and seeing a future with a sure sense that one part of it will include reminders of one's hometown.

Gratitude shines a pinpoint of light in
dark nights of doubt and disappointment.

Enduring friendships continue to fascinate and feed me. I recall those early days in Clarion and subsequent years as rings in the trunk of a tree. One can count the rings and telescope the years. Friendship grows ever so gradually and leaves a circle of memories that fill out the years of our lives. Memories are generally emotionally laden and unifying experiences. They remind us of our need for each other. We never really grow out of the dependency with which we enter this world. We cannot grow ourselves into human beings without leaning on and learning from others. We may be more aware of our seamless connections to humanity during those times when we felt left out or at least overlooked. I suppose having felt this way many times has enabled me to see and reach out to include those who seem excluded or are marginalized. My athletic ability and allied opportunities for status and success have helped me open doors for those shut out or only reluctantly let in. During playground days when I was selected to choose up sides, I began by choosing the lesser ability players, never forgetting where I came from. I learned there are many ways to win in life. Sometimes being a winner means being willing to lose on one end of life to make a difference at the other end. The other end is often helping someone step inside the group so they can occupy a place denied them many times earlier.

Belonging is often the antidote to one's longing to be someone who matters enough to be included. The inclusion can be simply a smile and pleasant greeting. A small act of kindness is at least a simple form of consideration that can brighten an otherwise dreary day. The recognition may be a simple sign of being noticed. For the deeply lonely, existence itself is disquieting and a dubious state of being. It is surprising how a small invitation to do something can release a person from the stranglehold of others' seeming indifference. To the discouraged and defeated, much energy is expended simply keeping life together. Being admitted into another's space is an accommodation that makes us feel more at home with ourselves. Being at home in our own space enables us to invite others to join us. We are not completely without our doubts about ourselves, but we gradually learn ways of befriending others and making friends with ourselves.

Believing we have something to offer is generally the initial step in building friendships. We introduce ourselves with small, calculated steps. We don't want to risk too much before surveying the landscape. As in learning to walk, one must learn to stand before taking a step. Encouragement is a set of open arms and a voice, "Come to Mommy." The encouragement of a loving and recognizable entity is all the assurance we need. We cross a space in a halting movement and an upright position. We are on our own. Yet, we feel capable of taking a chance on ourselves. Friendship often begins with small steps taken with encouragement toward another.

We are more likely to help someone learn to walk if we have already learned ourselves. Similarly, we are more likely to be sensitive to conditions of the heart if we have experienced heartache. We are more likely to take a chance being a welcoming spirit to those who have been dismissed or disregarded if we recall instances when we have risked something and learned to deal with rejection. We learn it is a temporary condition that passes like the time of day. It is easier to be hospitable if we have already withstood the temptation to protect ourselves from further hurt. We give others a second chance because we know life in all its main parts requires perseverance and tenacity. Little comes to us without our taking and passing tests of strength and endurance.

Many moves had taught me what it takes to enter the inner circle. I was left emotionally disposed to take in those who have been left out. As class president responsible for selecting persons to make things happen, I made it a point to select people who were unlikely to be given responsible roles. I increased the likelihood of their success by giving them well-defined tasks and frequent opportunities to report on their progress. My joy was in choosing and providing repeated opportunities to recognize success. I was elated to learn that those who generally stood on the sidelines or were nowhere to be seen, outperformed those who would have likely been the more proven choices. People rise to what they can be and do when someone from the inner circle believes they are more than meets the eye. Teamwork and team spirit are great levelers when it comes to sports. Success is a jointly conceived and cooperatively achieved outcome.

These same qualities are equally important off the field and produce similar results. In many instances, a desired performance demands collaborative rather than competitive attitudes and skills. Some of my classmates wanted a chance to demonstrate what they could do, but they lacked the confidence and assertiveness to make themselves known. They had been accustomed to standing in the shadows and watching others take the lead. Yet, they were ready to be asked and willing to contribute to projects that were organized around common objectives. They wanted to be included and recognized for having something to offer. I could afford to be a risk taker by inviting them into groups where I already belonged and was accepted. People had taken a chance on me. They did not gamble much initially;

they were not interested in big payoffs. They wanted to learn something of my potential to produce superior results in small matters and in a limited way, big dividends. I learned to make small and responsible contributions to the success of various enterprises. Success and recognition are cumulative. Once a person is seen, they are seldom overlooked. Once accounted for, a person is put on the ledger for life.

Gratitude looks through the lens of appreciation.

Over subsequent years my parents did not move again. I still have bouts with loneliness. There are times when I still feel adrift. Having a hometown does provide a place to anchor one's sense of belonging regardless of the distance one sails from port. Geography has separated me from my classmates over the years. But distance evaporates when memories of togetherness and bonds of simple pleasures and shared disappointment bridge it. We can catch glimpses of our past by returning to places where we stood together and learned life produces precious keepsakes.

Friendships do teach us we really cannot be separated from those we hold in our hearts. There is a vast place where those once-in-a-lifetime experiences and feelings can never be replicated regardless of how long we live or what we do. There is something magic about those years. We all knew something of loneliness, but most often it consisted of short bouts of indecision about how we thought about ourselves as well as what others thought of us.

I may have been more sensitive to this condition because I had frequently been the new kid on the block. I can recall feeling like a dislocated person in a strange land. I remember how small gestures of welcome swelled into wholesale expressions of acceptance. Now, fifty years later, I see with eyes of gratitude and listen to the voices reassuring me that my life has been a source of gratitude for others, too.

The cheerleader, the left tackle, and the right halfback are deceased. I am no less compensated, but less complete, because they too early preceded me in death. Death cannot separate us from the bonds of thankfulness and the rich rewards of remembrances. I can recall the simple activities and events that sent us down a similar path in life. They became for me genuine and gratuitous experiences of belonging.

I recently revisited the neighborhoods that gave me the space and place to grow. I began to unfold the map of storied memories and locate the people who are sources of gratitude to this day. Passing through the neighborhoods reminded me a hometown is much more than a location on the face of planet Earth. I could still mentally open the doors of my best friends' homes, go inside, and know my way around. The faces and spaces helped me retrace and assemble the history of an appreciated past. The homes also reminded me that longevity resides in our minds and is a gift of the heart. I came back to more than people assembled around a name on a map and a plot of land populated by 3,200 people. A hometown is comprised of people who hold one another together and collectively build a vision and foothold in our future.

Waves of gratitude spilled over me as I recalled borders that once kept me out but were stripped away to include me. These people *raised* me from isolation and alienation. Fifty years later I can look back and see with the eyes of gratitude and reconstruct the content of conversations that contributed to our growth as friends. They could not have known then how they lifted me out of the dark side of self-doubts into the secure assurances of friendship. Yet, relationships stretch in both directions and reach out beyond the initial point of contacts. We are social beings. We need more than ourselves to be truly invested in life. And once deeply invested, we are generously endowed and reimbursed. Lifelong investments continue to produce dividends, compounded annually, way into the future.

We do not have to move from one town to another to know loneliness. We have all been passed over in our quest to be accepted and belong. We have all longed to be included and been denied an opening. We have all taken a chance on others and been rebuffed. Thankfully, we all know what it feels like when someone steps out of the crowd, sees us, and invites us to join the group. We know the exhilaration of being included in making decisions, being admired, respected, and appreciated for our contributions. We treasure the time when we have been singled out as someone unique who has something to offer and have been invited to offer it. We prize the occasions when we could speak with authority and stand our ground because experience and certainty are our best friends. We are gladdened, having been a special piece of life for others, helping them pick up the pieces of their lives. We know what it feels like to be broken and made whole again, what it is to be locked out of the place we call home and have someone open the door. Life bounces us up and down, but we learn resilience. Life knocks us on the head, but we learn toughness. Life pokes away at our shortcomings, but we learn to poke back.

Gratitude harvests positive conclusions.

I am grateful I have a hometown to go back to. It isn't the place it used to be. In some ways it is just a crossroads between other towns. Like towns nearby, it has paved blocks lined with residences and an assorted collection of inhabitants. Not much distinguishes it from other geographically occupied spaces on Earth. Yet, to go there is to make an appointment with the past and an opportunity to interview my memories. I occasionally meet someone I know and who knew me then and when. They are thankful reminders of where I came from and telltale signs of ways I have changed.

On the one hand, there is enough tucked away in my past to remind me that part of me still belongs there. On the other hand, I realize we are meeting on different terms and cannot belong to one another again. I occasionally attend a traditional event, a community celebration, or a class reunion to jumpstart my feelings of nostalgia and happy times. People who still know my name offer small gestures of welcome. Hearing them say my name connects me with other appreciations of having been known and now remembered. We are members of a loosely knit family sewn at the seams of our common humanity. We visit at the fringes of a friendship, but no matter, it is at the edges that we live a good part of our lives.

Gratitude refurbishes the past with sparkling observations.

The past informed our minds, formed our hearts, and continues to shape our future. The friendships that gave us a reason to get up each day and build a future are often the forerunners of gratitude. We have given and have been given to. Recalling the ways serves as a catalyst for rediscovering something that was important and life-defining. Gratitude for having each other contributed to simple exchanges of something valued. We vaguely realize each of us is giving away something of ourselves and nothing was lost in the transaction. We are often surprised to learn how much we have to give away without being depleted. Friendship is not about cost accounting, nor is it about the arithmetic of addition and subtraction. Friendship is anchored in time-giving and space-sharing. It takes time to make a relationship and space to welcome another.

I am filled with gratitude when I look backward and remember rebirths and transforming benefits of friendship. I realize those who cultivate friendship make an ever-present investment in their own and others' happiness. It may begin in a place where we originally felt abandoned, displaced, and alone. It may start in a chance meeting and a chance remark. It may begin where and when we are least prepared to offer or accept it.

To be sure, friendship is not something we should take lightly or offer trivially. True and enduring friendships remind us we are bound together through mutual benefits of caring, concern, and support. Friends are bound by common expectations, lovingly chosen adherences, and faithfully fulfilled understandings. There is a give-and-take built into friendship that favors wholesale acceptance and appreciation. What we do in the name of friendship is collected and distributed over the vast territory called we and us. What we give and receive is multiplied a hundred-fold. Friendship is like a magic wand we wave across all of humanity. It transforms what would otherwise be plain and ordinary. We might choose to move from one location to another. However, there will always be a place in our hearts where friends have taken up residence, and at least occasionally show up in our wonderings, our imaginings, and our appreciations. There is more to learn and more to live when friends are good company and companions who travel with us to our varied destinations. Friendship, like gratitude, is a restless spirit that goes wherever kindness

needs a boost and consideration an affirmation. Like gratitude, friendship rejoices with what it offers and celebrates
with what it receives.

REFLECTION TODAY

Most things in life are defined for us. We learn to live
within boundaries established by supplied definitions. We
can choose to push out those boundaries. We may test the
limits as long as other people give us permission to do so.

Friendship is a special relationship defined by the persons who decide to make it so. Friend is a name we give to
someone, and like any other name, it does not begin to say
everything about what it stands for or claims to be. There
is some elasticity in our definition of friendship. We can
stretch its definition to include a variety of relationships,
variously encountered, committed and lived. It is generally
easier to define a friendship by taking a look at one through
the lens of experience. We often speak of the experience as
"making a friend" and "being a friend." These phrases seem
to encapsulate the inner workings of a friendship.

Reach out and take hold of the hands of a person you
regard as a "close" friend. Close refers not to physical space
but rather to psychological space. This is a person you hold
dear regardless of the geographical distance that separates
you. Once standing close to one another and facing each
other, look into the eyes of this person, and recall what you
have seen together and in one another that makes for the
special relationship you call friendship. Then step back so
you can see the entire person. Now pay attention to all the
other ways you have come to know one another. How have
hearing, smelling, tasting, touching, and posturing served
as instruments for knowing, understanding, believing, and
behaving? Use your observations to define your friendship,
that is, what it means to be a friend and to have a friend.

Now consider the significance of gratitude in forming and sustaining this friendship. How has what you have
given and been given served to create a wellspring of gratitude you can draw upon to satisfy your thirst to be a friend
and have a friend? How has gratitude served as a mainstay
in your relationship and been the midwife of what has been
born in your relationship?

REFLECTION TOMORROW

Not all relationships result in a friendship. We have
many casual, social acquaintances. We are content to let
some people move in and out of our lives without much
thought about building a friendship. We enjoy our occasional encounters and the conversations that ensue. We are
interested in their lives but aren't inclined to become part
of them.

We also have many simple associations. These generally occur in work situations. Our work tends to define the
associative relationship. We may have occasion to chitchat
about our lives outside of work, but the casual exchanges
are not intended to produce anything more than the collaborative attitude our jobs require of us. We don't have any
expectation that what we know about each other and share
with one another will likely lead to anything permanent.

Identify a person who fits one or the other of these two
relationships. Use this relationship to discover characteristics that serve to distinguish between friendship and an
acquaintance or associative relationship. Compare what
you learned about the characteristics of friendship and
those that define an acquaintance and/or associate.

What characteristics seem to most sharply differenti-
ate these less involved relationships from friendships?

What friendship characteristics seem to overlap with those that define the way we deal with these less permanent relationships?

What friendship characteristic would you most likely draw upon if you wanted to gradually make and be a friend of an acquaintance or an associate?

How might gratitude contribute to the transition from an acquaintanceship or association to a friendship?

CHAPTER 4

Work

*Gratitude elevates dignity and
heralds the results of work.*

We all grew up doing something. We cannot sit idly by and become something worthy of ourselves and respected by others. We gradually grow and are defined by how we respond to others' expectations. We make ourselves into a story by making something of what we do. Each day we know we are supposed to be something more. We work at writing a better story.

During my teen-aged years working in my father's bakery, I became a character in his story. Work was a defining characteristic of his story, and it was to become one of mine. At first I was given tasks that did not require much skill. These tasks did not include working with or alongside my dad or the other two bakers, and they certainly weren't glamorous. At the outset they were confined to scraping and washing pans, cleaning equipment, and scraping and preparing areas on the workbench for other operations. I also prepared items to be placed in the pastry display case. These mundane activities did release the bakers to prepare the actual products to be purchased by customers. I could see how I was contributing to this end.

My dad frequently reminded me of my contributions with pertinent observations and appreciative remarks. He eventually invited me to work alongside the other bakers. At first it was to simply make or assemble some part of a particular product; I might slice a section of dough from a larger batch, form it, weigh it, and run it through a press that cut it into cubes. Later I learned to roll cubes into balls that, after being placed in a proof box to raise, were flattened, raised again, and baked as hamburger buns. My dad was the oven man because he had a keen eye for color and a deft hand for texture. I was proving myself through a pre-planned induction into more responsible roles.

My most responsible and prized role was repeated between 4:30 and 6:30 a.m. weekdays and 2:00 and 7:00 a.m. Saturdays. I was the person who fried and glazed the donuts. This operation left a distinctive and appetizing fragrance on my clothing. My classmates occasionally smelled this enticing scent on days when I went directly to school. It encouraged them to make the bakery a lunch-hour destination. Our bakery was widely known outside our community for raised, glazed donuts. Our location, a half block off the main drag and Highway 3, became a traveler's junction for those coming home or going somewhere else.

I was proud of being solely responsible for preparing the lightly browned, flakey, and scrumptious glazed donuts. I was also known as the only person who could fry, glaze, and pan the donuts for sale as an uninterrupted and artful process. The process began when one baker rolled a batch of dough and used a round cutter with a tube in the middle to cut out donuts. He would place rows of formed dough in a steamy "proof box" to raise. He then put the raised dough on a rack for me to retrieve. My first task was to place one and a half dozen raw donuts on a metal screen platform.

Placement was a challenging process that entailed using both hands. The left hand was used to gently lift one edge of the donut, transferring it to my right hand, with which I delicately laid it on a metal mesh tray, gradually removing my right hand by letting my fingernails drag along the tray to ensure the raised remained raised. The two handles on the left and right edges of the tray were of sufficient length to keep my hands out of the hot oil.

My claim to fame was being able to put a tray of raw donuts in the fryer, glaze the donuts that had been previously fried, and put them on a drying rack before having to turn the donuts in the fryer. Then, returning to the fryer, I turned the donuts over with wooden sticks, stacked previously dried glazed donuts on a store-display pan, and retrieved another pan of unfried donuts before pulling the original batch of donuts from the fryer. Then the frying/glazing process began all over again. The real trick was to keep the donuts the same appealing color, bathe them in glaze while they were still hot, and maintain the donuts' exquisite texture as the quality of the grease changed, due to the flour on the exterior of the dough.

Gratitude delights in the esteem of others.

Through all this work experience during my high school years, I came to appreciate the gradual way we master a task and acquire competence through repetition and practice. We begin to grow capabilities through small, incremental, and seemingly insignificant steps. Like a child learning to walk, the initial stages seem like clumsy, tangled movements. Actually they are preparing the body to contribute to various tasks, each of which eventually combines and integrates with others to form a function we refer to as walking. Initially I also learned through some trial and error, gradually acquiring and honing the necessary skills. What began as mental images and the sequencing of selectively precise behaviors eventually became routines and habits performed smoothly and accurately without conscious thought. Competence was a subtle collection of distinctions and discoveries all woven together to produce an accomplished outcome. These abilities also were forerunners of complementary attitudes and values. What we do affects who we become. Character is the summation of our longings, strivings, and accomplishments. We want to make good on what is possible and ordained.

Comparing and admiring the consistency of my results with others' work-related accomplishments amplified the satisfaction of my work, as did affirmations from the other bakers — the cohort to which I now belonged. My developing work ethic was part of the process for making my story. I knew I was meant to be something more.

Gratitude revels in what we have learned to do.

I learned to be grateful for my hands during our family's summer visits to my father's childhood home. I was still at a tender age when my grandmother, seated at the kitchen table, would occasionally ask me to hold out my hands. She would place them in her hands and gently rub my palms. Silently turning my hands over and over several times, she would stroke my fingers and bend them gently into an accepting grasp. It was as though she was trying to help me get in touch with something sacred and sublime. She did not have a crystal ball, but I knew she was preparing me to fathom something beyond this time and place. The silence was only broken when she was sure I had begun to grasp an understanding of what she wanted to reveal: something that would help me travel the distance between boyhood and manhood. She would raise my hands up from her lap, wait for my eyes to meet hers, and say, "These are worker hands." I knew from her voice and the quiet moments preceding this revelation that it was meant to be the ultimate compliment and intended to be a preview of future achievements. Worker hands were an entrustment and a legacy to be honored and cherished. They were to be standard bearing instruments and reliable resources for creating a future yet to be imagined.

I was being invited to recognize the ennobling virtue of work and its power to secure the future. I was to understand my role in perpetuating a legacy of hard work and appreciate the sacrifices of those who had gone before me. The work-centered values and tenacious adherence to hard work were not just a means to an end. Work had inherent value. It was the birthright of all who originally grew their story on the American frontier. As the oldest of five boys, I was to be the standard-bearer for those who would use work to realize a future marked by progress and prosperity. Those who own the past can use it to build a better future. We are stewards of ambition who draw upon it to create something new.

Gratitude inspires one generation's contributions to the next.

Hands can be used to take hold of an ideal and place it in the hands of the next generation. My grandmother was inducting me into a way of thinking about and looking at the world, a way of listening to the biddings of the future, and a way of deciding what one will pay to be secure in it. Hands are made for work. They are representations and

advocates for the rest of what we bring to making a difference. And work is a celebration of what one can do. It is the
forerunner of what we become and value as adults.

Gratitude preserves the indispensable heritage of each generation.

Our DNA tells us one story and we are disposed to live
it. Our heritage offers us another story and we are inclined
to take it seriously. We generally put both our DNA and
our heritage in the making of our own story. This has certainly been true for me. I have been greatly influenced by
the imprint of history, and my genes have had to make the
accommodations. I learned hard work was the mainstay of
my grandparents' generation. It was prized, almost idol-
ized. It was practically all some people knew. There were
few restful interludes between dawn and dusk. Work was
not just putting bread on the table and a roof over one's
head. Work was a virtue intended to be honored by everyone. No one was to be excused. Everyone was expected to
carry his or her own load. Those who were idle became a
load for others to lift.

People lived lives of scarcity, necessity, and sufficiency.
Nothing material was wasted. Time was painstakingly
invested in labor. Work was so important that it became
a validation of one's worth. A good worker was worth his
weight in gold. A good worker was the salt of the earth.
My father and two other bakers reinforced my grandmother's tender appraisal and gentle reminders about the
relationship between hands and the virtue of work. The
hand-demonstrative character of a baker's work drove
home the message and validated the messenger.

Gratitude appreciates wisdom and distills the counsel of persons we respect.

Year upon year the favorable and consistent repetition of these attitudes and values prepared me to take my place among those who had braved and survived the struggles of the frontier. They faced off against and did battle with the harsh and stark realities of the Depression. Victories did not come without some wounds and casualties. Fear of the future, its uncertainty and instability, may have been the major casualty. Wounds were treated with the medicinal qualities of hard work. I was not left untouched by the trauma of these battles. Work became a bedrock value, and excelling at work became a mantra for my life. I acquired worker attitudes, forged worker ideals, and groomed myself as a worker. I was productive and proficient. Growing competent and competitive was a way of thinking about and doing life. I gradually came to the realization that my success was built upon the foundation of other people's skills, their recognition, affirmation, and thankfulness for what I could do. I was proving myself in the world where the coin of the realm was work.

Gratitude sustains, preserves, and honors.

My accomplishments were initially rooted in proving myself to others. I would strive to exceed others' expectations and did not surrender to compromises. I wanted to do my best and be the best. I was possessed with a desire to make my way into the adult world where good work was the admission price to approval and success.

My ambition and achievements were acknowledged and rewarded with prized acceptance and greater trust and responsibility. Others were grateful for me and me for them. This reciprocity became a stable influence in my life. Soon the inclusion in something that mattered was a sufficient incentive to grow me into something more. My desire for additional competence no longer depended upon favorable appraisals of my work and celebratory remarks about my promise. I stood as a man among men. There was a growing certainty about the value of work, but a complementary understanding that work was not the only path to self-esteem and self-worth. I began to understand while my life was anchored in distinguishing work-related standards, there were other ways to grow a deeper understanding of self and a more expansive view of life. I began to be grateful for who I was becoming aside from the contributions I could make with "worker hands." While there is something more basic and more enduring in the human spirit than work, work does serve to mediate the transformative power of other outlets for growth. It is a feeling that transcends the momentary and fleeting satisfaction of a job well done. It is a spirit that tells us to listen to life and learn the lessons leisure can teach us.

Gratitude renews the conversation we have with ourselves.

I am grateful for those who saw something unique in me, who taught me what they knew and were sure I could do it. I initially had reason to be grateful because they believed in me more than I believed in myself. I am now grateful that achievements in one sector of life have become a foothold for stepping up to other challenges of living. Gratitude is knowing we have something to offer that transcends merely getting things done. We are worth much more than what we can do. We possess a spirit that welcomes our participation in the intangibles of beauty and rhythm of life itself.

Work has been and continues to be a way of spending part of my life. It has been an investment in others that has daily paid dividends for me and them. We cannot always bank on doing precisely what we want and what others need from us. But we can make our best effort live up to the essence of our humanity and bow before a spirit that unites us to something larger than ourselves. Gratitude enters the picture because work is both a product and a by-product of finding something meaningful to do, to believe in, and give ourselves to. We need goals and the realization of them. We need to think beyond where we stand and prepare ourselves to go there. We need to come to some understanding of our place in the world and give something permanent to our having been here.

Gratitude builds bridges between our desire and ability to better humankind.

I am grateful I have had mentors who taught me the value of work and the benefits of making what I did matter. However, in retrospect, I believe this conviction may have been too deeply entrenched in duty rather than embedded in growth. Work became more than the backbone for standing up to the world and facing down its demands. I became too dedicated to work as the ultimate good, a crowning achievement, and a penultimate definition of self. There was not a good balance between work as a way of making a living and leisure as a growing interiority that depends upon other forms of nourishment. Work in and of itself does have redeeming and transformative possibilities, but so does leisure, as it lifts the human spirit beyond the boundaries set by habit, routine, and necessity.

I am grateful for a college education, particularly my introduction to the liberal arts, wherein I learned from turning pages, taking notes, writing papers, grasping ideas, and appropriating the images that have stood the test of time and have served as instruments for acquiring and preserving our heritage. My hands were freed from hard physical labor by the hands and toil of my grandparents. Their minds were not idle, but they were seldom free to look beyond the immediate circumstances and demands of life. Their work was no less worthy, only differed in kind, emphasis, and expression. Their work provided me the scaffolding I stand on to reach higher. Their achievements and viewpoints have provided me with the desire and tools to live beyond the past, to see beyond the immediate, and to take charge of the future.

Gratitude is a force that connects us across generations and inspires us to draw up the strength, courage, and hopes of our ancestors. Were it not for one generation laying the groundwork, through industriousness, resourcefulness, and ingenuity, we would merely repeat what has been thought and done before them. We would be subjects of the past and servants of a present with little more to commend it. But life in America has been a seamless garment. It is woven to clothe each generation with inspiration, ambition, and hopes that supersede the past, illumine the present, and forge a future. The garment is sewn from a fabric that stretches so it can embody the strivings of the entrepreneur, the creativity and novelty of the artist, and the intellectual and expansive property of the scientist, judge, lawmaker, and spiritual mentor.

My dad was not deliberately intent upon teaching me gratitude by training me in the ways and habits of work. Work was an indirect path to gratitude for me and a source of security for him. He was conspicuously grateful we were able to work together and dignify the intangibles that define and distinguish a father-and-son relationship. We were able to share a location that was more than a place to work. Two positions were melded into a single purpose. Today few adolescents actually know or understand what their fathers do when they leave for work. I did. And so much more.

I say "so much more" because the bakery was a place where businessmen congregated and newspaper boys hung out, folded papers, and ate glazed donuts between 5 a.m. and 7 a.m. every morning. I could observe the ways other men regarded my dad. I eavesdropped on conversations about business, politics, community pride, and economic improvements. I stood inside a circle of influence and listened to conversations aimed at progress. I listened to exchanges that revealed the mutual esteem and wholesome camaraderie that framed community and set the agenda for the future. People of goodwill, loyalty, helpfulness, and caring structured relationships. Leaders were good neighbors who brought people together to form and construct a corporate identity and shape a future. I met leaders in the early hours of the morning. I learned how to be a good neighbor by acting upon what I heard and appreciating my privileged look into the future.

Gratitude evolves from a gradual appreciation of one another.

I continue to be grateful to have known my dad as other men knew him. He stood tall in my mind. He became an ever-present reminder of the ideals that define our humanity and equip us to be something more than ourselves. I am grateful for having been a participant in a workplace where I was schooled in the elements of critical thinking and given permission to think creatively. I am grateful to have been included among men when I was still a boy, to be respectfully addressed and occasionally invited to express my opinion. I had opportunities to foresee the beginnings of change for our small town and track the progress of an idea.

I am also grateful I grew up in the bakery because it taught me I didn't want to be a baker. I am grateful the people in this small circle of influence expected me to go to college. I had my own unexpressed misgivings, but they were gradually overcome as opportunities and requirements. unfolded. I did have thoughts about giving up on others' expectations during my freshman year. However, I could not imagine fielding the questions, facing the embarrassment, and dealing with the uncertainties of an alternative future.

Gratitude does claim part of our future, as we feel somewhat beholden to those who have placed their faith in us and want us to realize the possibilities they see in us. Gratitude gives us an inch, but we feel obliged to go a mile. The mile is not just a matter of distance and geography. The mile is an attitude that stretches us beyond what we believe about ourselves and insists we can be everything others imagine. It is not an easy road to travel because we lack their hindsight and the complementary benefits of foresight. We are asked to trust what we do not know and hope with a feeble sense of confidence. We go forward and backward with an awkward, messy, and uneasy suspicion they may be right. Gratefully I found them so.

Gratitude wraps us in a quilt sewn from our labor.

REFLECTION TODAY

Reflect upon something you are particularly grateful you can do, something that is a source of considerable satisfaction and an accomplishment admired by others. Think of one person who was most influential in the realization of this powerfully held achievement. This person supported and encouraged you when you doubted yourself or when you lacked the discipline to forge ahead. This person celebrated increments of progress with you and kept you fixed and focused on your goal. Use the answers to these observations to assemble thoughts that give you reason to be grateful for this person. Summon the images that contribute to feelings of gratitude and reconnect you to the person who was an instrument of imagination, encouragement, and support. Find an outlet for acting out your thoughts and feelings so others know the power of gratitude in your life.

REFLECTION TOMORROW

Reflect upon some quality (characteristic or virtue) you admire in yourself. This defining quality is a mark of distinction in your life. Recall a person who was particularly struck by the significance and benefit of this self-acclaimed quality. This person has supported and encouraged you to cultivate this quality in ways that are uniquely you. How has this self-esteemed quality become a "loving this is who I am" distinction in your life? How have others been served and blessed because the expressions of this quality have been a life-giving experience for them? How has the power of gratitude helped you remain faithful to this quality and to trust it in your relationship with others?

CHAPTER 5

Hospitality

Gratitude begins at home.

Our mother creates our first dwelling place in her body. Though we have no street or mailing address, she lets everyone know where to find us. In time, there is no doubt about our location and to whom we belong. Our mother feeds us with all we need to grow ourselves into something worthy of the blessing. Hospitality becomes a connection, a partnership if you will, between nature and nurture. She uses her body to cooperate with nature and her love to nurture the environment where we reside. A mother is a gateway to hospitality.

We are born with two social behaviors and one emotion: We can cry and suck. When these two behaviors are frustrated, we get angry. We depend upon hospitality, the caring, attention, and concern of another, to attend to these behaviors. We would not last long were it not for a provider or family of providers. By definition, a person is a member of both.

The family may consist of various configurations. Regardless of the membership, it functions as a primary socialization unit in our society, teaching us what it means to be family and how to behave as responsible members of it. The family unit helps us define who I am and who I am not. We learn what is acceptable to do and what is inappropriate. We gradually build a world inside that connects us to a world outside, and we learn to transact business between these two worlds. Our parents help us to sift through all the variations of what it means to be me and what is not me. We gradually learn to take responsibility for what distinguishes between where I end and others begin.

The family serves as the center of our activities and our conclusions about the purpose and meaning of life. Gathering, sitting down, and conversing together during a family meal can be a powerful socialization activity. Exchanging thoughts, feelings, and actions becomes the basis for relationship-building attitudes and interpersonal management skills. This education occurs by way of intention and by osmosis. We become persons with a history and build a life by looking back from where we have been and imagining where we can go. We are held together by rituals, customs, and conversations that define the boundaries of who we are to one another.

The family does not exist in isolation from others. Families make room for others who matter. We take them in and make space for them in the narrative of our lives. We learn about assumptions that keep our world small. Members of other families may be relatives or neighbors living in physical proximity. They may be friends and associates who come in and out of the family. We are most hospitable to persons who are most like us, those who share similar attitudes and values. They are the persons who are most likely to join us at table, where we share stories and develop narratives that connect us to distinctive and common forms of expression. Some become welcome guests of our hearts and soul mates as traditions bind us to one another.

Family life gradually transforms our attitude and outlook toward life. We come to understand and pledge ourselves to what it means to be family. Today we hear persons from all walks of life and differing persuasions talking about family values. The conversation includes those who have chosen lifestyles that challenge the traditional family unit of a father, mother, and children. Others believe sacred family values are being undermined by those who refuse to accept the traditional tenets of faith-based religious groups.

The debate hinges on many assumptions about the role of family life; the role and responsibilities, the contributions of its members, and the ultimate benefits of a stable family unit in a mobile society. Sociologists, anthropologists, psychologists, and economists offer varying interpretations, explanations, and assessments of the current situation. Many acknowledge it is important for children to have an adult male and adult female role model. Learning to be masculine or feminine, and how to negotiate genetic, developmental, and cultural influences are typically learned better in an emotionally trustworthy, intellectually stimulating, socially healthy, and spiritually vibrant family. Children who grow up in these arrangements are made to feel and think positively about themselves and are likely to succeed as responsible and productive members of society. They will most likely become the parents of families much like their own. This is not to say some children may achieve similar results in other family configurations. Many do believe all the essential conditions for favorable growth and development can be found in nontraditional families.

Gratitude educates and enlightens the heart.

My wife and I are grateful we grew up in traditional families. We are likely to be partial to this arrangement because we did not know anything else. We have cherished and celebrated the ways we were raised by adopting many attitudes and duplicating many child-rearing practices of our parents. Our decision to begin making our life together as a family provider and homemaker is the most telling sign of our parents' influence. Our fathers left the home each day to earn a living while moms stayed home to make a living.

We talked at length about making this choice. We knew it would delay our having many things two-income couples have. Fortunately, we were able to become friends with other couples who had made the same decision. Like us, they could recall how they felt knowing their mothers would be at home while they were away at school and would be there when they returned. Mom was a stable figure who often greeted our arrival with homemade treats. We could have our fill of both worlds: have our cake and eat it too. At times, we shared the joy and the cake with classmates. They were often friends who lived in our neighborhood and were included in our after-school activities. These feelings and realizations provided material for discussions about novel, favorite, and homemade traditions that grew up around family life and family outings. Our decisions to grow our families as we had grown up became the impetus for joint family gatherings.

Gratitude anchors itself in reliable surroundings.

Our home was not confined to a physical dwelling. It also served as a meeting place to socialize with other couples, and we wanted our children to have an expanded experience of other families. Special holidays and traditionally celebrated family events became opportunities to share our stories, model our shared values, and enrich one another's lives.

Each family brought its history to these celebratory events. Our children could experience our collective commitment to similar values. Table conversation prompted and nourished the development of our extended family when we sat down together. Each family brought something to share to satisfy our appetite for food and belonging. Life involved becoming something larger than ourselves. Parents would keep lifelines open between family gatherings with telephone conversations and mid-day coffee visits that became the ingredients for continuity, stability, and commitment. The opening and closing of events in our lives serve as pronouncements for who we are to one another and invitations to extend what we already have.

We were fortunate to purchase a house two blocks from the school our children attended. They could come home for lunch and have a brief respite from classroom-structured activities. Coming home enlarged the menu options in a settled and inviting atmosphere and furnished something more than nourishment for the body. Generally, lunchtime at home included inquiries and conversations about events at school. At an early age, children are receptive to such inquiries and readily share their day. These conversations often became the centerpiece of our evening meal.

Our parents had taught us the evening meal could be a classroom for teaching family values and goals. We sat down at approximately the same time every evening. This was a sacred time, seldom breached by adults, even at the cost of being unable to attend other adult social gatherings. The evening meal featured the exchange of stories played out in our lives that day. We reluctantly but occasionally adjusted mealtime to accommodate school-sponsored activities, but seldom did we let anything else disrupt this family dynamic. Since our mealtime practice began early in their lives, our children grew up learning to listen and to wait for their turn, and they accepted this time as an opportunity rather than an expectation. The habit was well-formed before they got to the stage where the question, "What happened at school today?" could be or would be answered, "Nothing" or "Not much." Actually, the question was seldom asked because conversation at supper was a naturally occurring and free-flowing event.

Gratitude becomes an acquired way of thinking and living.

The evening meal was also a time for teaching family values, a time for our children to listen to exchanges between their mom and dad. These alternating remarks often included the basis for making decisions, standards for treating people, and criteria for planning the future. The conversation was not an overt way to teach values, which are often learned by being gradually absorbed into the mainstream of one's thinking and acting. That is not to say there were not occasions when questions were used to probe a thought and reinforce a value or endorse an insight. There were times when we were exacting about what we believed and uncompromising about appropriate behaviors.

Gratitude makes way for consistency and constancy.

I would go to work shortly before the children went to school and arrive home a couple of hours after they did. I was a college professor, so my evenings included preparing lectures and reading student papers. The material for these activities was transported in an aged, leather briefcase that also served as a treasure chest. My walk home from campus occasionally included purchases at a grocery store on College Hill, a commercial area where about a dozen merchants occupied a two-block incline leading to the pillared entrance to the campus. These businesses served the neighborhood and students with the essentials of daily life. With thoughts of our children in mind, I sometimes added their favorite treats to the grocery list. I would stow this purchase in my briefcase, envisioning their excitement when one of them was invited to go to my study after supper and bring my briefcase to the table. Of all the little planned and unplanned happenings, being invited to get my briefcase is one our children remember most fondly.

This was a welcomed request because it always meant some kind of sweet treat. One treat surpassed all others: spice drops — soft, sugar-coated, dome-like candies that come in several colors. I would delay the actual delivery of the goodies by creating three rows, one for each child, each row consisting of one spice drop of each color and flavor. The lineup might be orange, green, red, purple, white, and yellow. Generally, one of each color was put in the row before a second color was added. Each of the three rows contained the same number of spice drops, arranged in the same order. Suspense was mixed with glee. This sequence was predictable. However, on some occasions, some colors might be duplicated and others omitted. There were some groans when there were two of one color because that meant some color/flavor had been excluded. The children always received the same number and accepted the number as a constant. Seldom did they, individually or collectively, ask for more. They learned to be grateful for what they received.

There is some virtue in gratitude that recognizes the limits of what we are given and asks for nothing more. The joy and fullness of gratitude can be diminished if our expectations or desires set the bar too high. Gratitude does not have a chance to make its presence known. Rather than attempting to approach the bar, gratitude steps back and disappointedly walks away. The lack of gratitude leads to disappointment, which frequently spreads out and washes up against other negative emotions. The tide recedes leaving one feeling at a loss.

Gratitude does not depend on always getting its way.

Unfortunately, many people do not sit around a table of plenty. For them, each day is a struggle between having and being enough. They must make the best of what they have. There is little in life to introduce and welcome them into gratitude when hope is dim or nonexistent. One's blessings, often taken for granted, need to become the basis for moving forward and generously reaching out to others. Then we can view the destitute as deserving the dignity of a better life. Without being moved by gratitude, substituting blame for compassion is a defense for doing nothing. This disposition makes it easy to forget the favorable circumstances of one's life and how others have contributed to one's prosperity and security. Strength and resolve are gifts to be appreciated and paid forward. They are to become marks of humility put in the service of humanity. Gratitude is easily overlooked by those who regard their success as the merited outcome of self-reliance.

At other times, we take for granted the way we are treated because we feel entitled to that treatment. We may have an exaggerated sense of our importance and become accustomed to being treated accordingly. We complain when we are not but don't take note when we are. We are all a little spoiled. We believe we know what is rightfully ours and see no reason to make a big thing of it when we are accorded what we deserve.

Gratitude prolongs a desirable condition while offsetting an undesirable one.

Gratitude is not prideful or haughty. It is simply accepting what is offered, appreciating the giver, and welcoming the gift, particularly when what is given is a gift from the heart. With true gratitude, there is no ledger sheet determining what is owed or what should be given. It does not depend upon tangibles to be given away and can be exchanged in the open market without consulting a financial adviser. Unlike greed, gratitude is not ambitious. It pauses to appreciate what one has and does not desire more than is needed. It thrives in the pleasure of the moment and, unlike greed, does not strive for more of everything.

The special relationship between food and hospitality offers some meaningful insights. For example, time is an essential ingredient; there must be enough of it to satisfy our hunger for something more than food on our plates. Our hearts and souls, as well as our bodies, long to be fed and nourished. We need the benefit of healthy servings of human interaction, which is a staple of life. Our meal must be flavored with the spice of wholesome conversation and healthy observations. Food and hospitality become bedfellows in families where members value one another. Then the welcome can be extended to others, and the invitation includes befriending gestures that make a meal a celebration. We learn how to entertain and become a guest by participating at a variety of family and social gatherings. Table fellowship becomes an experience with strong ties to ennobling bonds of affection.

We have told or listened to hundreds of stories while dining together. Food opens our mouths and our ears; we can simultaneously take in food and acquire food for thought. There is something enriching about tasting food and relishing life. We savor a good meal when we have an appetite for life.

Gratitude stretches and strengthens hospitality's foothold in our lives.

Belonging to a family is a transformative experience of hospitality. A redemptive spirit is woven into our story of togetherness. Somehow as the tale is told and retold, everyone in the story becomes more believable, accepted, and affirmed. The telling seems to soften the message and makes the participants more endearing. The stories invite us to become part of a shared experience. They are not just small talk but the culmination of things worth remembering and perpetuating. For others, they become a household invitation to feast on our stories, to dine at our table while learning about our lives. The stories have domestic origins but change as they travel from one household to another. They serve as prompts for guests to tell their stories, and the varied offerings widen our horizons and redefine our lives. We come to know and are known. We come to believe and are believed. We come to value and be valued.

REFLECTION TODAY

Everyone grows up in some kind of family arrangement. Everyone becomes a "someone" as a consequence of
being a member of a family. We like part of who we have
become because of the family we grew up in. At times, we
likely wish our family had been less influential in the way
we think of ourselves and the choices we have made.

Select some positive personality trait or desirable
life-directing value that you attribute to your parent(s) or
to your membership in a family. Trace the development of
this trait or value, as an extension of the way hospitality
became a fixture in the way you think or a habit in the way
you behave. Recall ways hospitality has helped fashion the
value or fortify the behavior. Note other ways hospitality
has become a powerful influence in the choices you make
and the person you are.

REFLECTION TOMORROW

Identify a personality trait you would like to better
define you. For example, you may want to think of yourself
and/or have others think of you as kinder and more patient,
understanding, or generous. How might you use the desire
to be a more hospitable person to strengthen your resolve
and increase the incidences of your behaving the way you
want to be regarded and experienced? Think of gratitude
as a reward you give yourself and/or the result of others
acknowledging your efforts. Do you begin to see gratitude is
both an incentive to grow and a reward for having grown?

CHAPTER 6

Serendipity

Gratitude can alter your life path.

Soon after I retired, people began asking me what I planned to do during retirement. They tended to think of retirement as being synonymous with travel and often suggested places I should visit. I would indicate I wasn't much for traveling, justifying myself by citing all the reasons for staying home and making more of life in my current surroundings. I cited the hassles of preparing to travel, the unexpected mishaps affecting even the best-laid plans, and the expense of going anywhere these days. They would point to self-help books loaded with suggestions to minimize all the problems I could muster for my position. Despite the point-counterpoint exchanges, I remained skeptical and a staunch advocate of staying put.

This was all true until my parents returned from a trip to Canada to revisit my father's past. My resistance was initially lowered by listening to their account of the people they met, the places they visited, and the greater appreciation of my father's heritage. I began to imagine it was possible to reduce the hassle by merely duplicating their plans and activities. With their pictures, maps, and personal accounts, they would provide the names of people, localities to visit, and ways to curtail expenses. We could retrace the events and drama with the benefit of their experience and enjoy the adventure without being subject to uncertainty. We could make a budget to curtail expenses. As the possibilities opened up, my reservations melted away.

I gradually became fascinated with resurrecting and duplicating their experience. I was particularly enamored with entering the places and imagining what took place in the spaces my ancestors had occupied. My father was especially good at creating images of the people and the times that defined their lives. He kept a detailed account of his and my mother's activities and delighted in describing the characteristics and lifestyle of those who were instrumental in making their trip a success. As my interest became more apparent, he gave me names of people to contact, pictures of places to see, and a historical account of my grandparents' activity in this area around the early twentieth century. We gradually collected all the information we needed to maximize the use of our time and make the most of the hospitality that had made their trip so memorable.

My grandfather, Lars, was a Lutheran Free Church minister, and the Canada trip became the impetus and basis for my father writing a family history. He writes:

> There was one thing in common with today, however, and that was a committee. It generally happens when history is recorded the committee gets the credit and no mention is made of who did the actual work. The committee built this church in 1905, the first church in the territory. Recorded church history does not identify Lars, the only skilled carpenter in the area.

Yet the old-timers told him Lars planned, laid out, and supervised the construction of this church. He single-handedly built the pulpit, altar, and altar rail.

Among all the incidents my father related after the trip, I was most curious about the church. My interest was probably peaked because I am an ordained permanent deacon in the Catholic Church. I read and proclaim the Gospel, give homilies, prepare and deliver intercessory prayers, and administer the cup during communion. These liturgical roles and ministerial functions served as connections to the pulpit, the altar, and communion rail my grandfather designed and crafted. A community of believers is built around these three invitations to faith and sources of grace. These sacred conventions and my curiosity eventually became the driving force for my decision to travel and ultimately spend time in the church. I hoped to reconnect with the spirit of those who came there to worship and make a home for family fellowship. My desire to participate in this activity is rooted in my belief that we are generative and transformative beings who leave deposits of our spirit wherever we make deep commitments to life and spend part of our life-energy on what is life-giving.

As a student of the Bible, my father found certain passages particularly meaningful and inspirational. From time to time, he would refer to them in conversations devoted to issues with moral overtones. His love of scripture introduced me to the spiritual foundation of my faith, his applications of scripture to practices I honor today. The coalescing of these attitudes and actions sealed the deal.

Gratitude prepares us to belong to something we cannot touch, but feel.

We arrived in Donalda, Alberta, Canada — the largest town in proximity to our primary destination, the Ferry Point Church. On the north side of the one-block-long main street was an information center/museum. We went inside to inquire about the location of the residence of Mrs. Dagny Norman, the most knowledgeable and hospitable person my parents had met some years earlier. She still lived in Donalda. When we described our wish to meet Mrs. Norman, our first host, the person at the information center, volunteered to call her. Mrs. Norman recognized the Froyen name, connected it with my parents, and invited us to come to her home. She was a delightful, gregarious person who generously engaged in the life of the community. Her remarks were filled with connections to people and prized relationships. She came across as combining the attributes of a good neighbor, a counselor, and a minister.

After regaling us with the history of the area and fortifying us with wonderful pastries and iced tea, Mrs. Norman suggested calling Don Saltvold, who immediately warmed to us and was curious about our mission. Upon learning our destination, he volunteered to escort us to the Ferry Point Church. Mrs. Norman and Mr. Saltvold invited us to begin our adventures early the next day. The trip would inform and form us as we crisscrossed the past and the present.

The road to the church was cut from several acres of grass and timber. Light filtered through a canopy of leaves casting shadows on the grass-covered pathway below. There, immediately before us, stood a stately, well-kept, white building whose spire was the only clue that it was a church rather than a rural one-room schoolhouse. We stepped across the threshold, where so many had crossed before us. We were participating in a very privileged moment in time, sensing this was to be a special convergence of the past and present. I wanted to seize the moment and hold onto it.

We were *crossing the threshold* with a reverence similar to that of those earlier worshippers. I imagined this space being filled with molecules of air that may have filled it ninety years ago. Who is to say that the air I breathed was not the same as that breathed by my grandparents? Or to imagine the air passing across my body did not once touch the skin of those who preceded me? Windows were opened to shower us with a cool gentle breeze. Maybe my uncles and aunt drew their first breaths on a day like this.

I began to look around. Although voices punctuated the silence, time seemed to stand still. The church is used occasionally for weddings and funerals. Like other public structures, its walls and bulletin boards were covered with faded announcements, Sunday school records, and miscellaneous bulletins. There seemed to be no pattern in the distribution of these items or any way to discern their significance. They had survived attempts to tidy the space and withstood the elements of time.

Standing like a sentinel just inside the front door was a stately cast-iron potbelly stove whose black exterior had long ago disappeared. Now the arched ribbing that formed the belly was attired with a rusty blanket of brown, blue, and gray. Two sturdy metal doors opened to distribute warmth and provide a way to later remove ashes. A stout metal ring encircled the belly immediately below the doors, a warning to anyone who might stand too close when stoking the fire. The flue separated the entrance area and the congregation's high-backed wooden chairs. The stove must have been a welcomed relief on bitter winter days, when people shook off the

cold and traded gestures of welcome. Gratitude must have
been a partner in these exchanges of fellowship.

Standing in the aisle that separated the seating accommodations for the congregation, I looked into the sanctuary
and was struck by a brightly painted white communion rail
located in front of a similarly painted altar. Rising from the
base of the altar were two sculpted columns connected by an
arched molding. Encased between the columns was a framed
print of the Good Shepherd. As the centerpiece for the sanctuary, it revealed the essence of the faith community, whose
members place their trust in a God who cares for them. As
his flock, they are gathered into his care and drawn to one
another by their common dependence on the fruits of the
land. Theirs is a tradition of seeing God's work all about
them and giving thanks for the bounty of their land.

Our hosts were particularly pleased to draw our attention to the pulpit, altar, and communion rail; they knew
my grandfather's hands had shaped these icons for worship. They were also proud that the organ, purchased by
the Luther League in 1910 for ninety-five dollars, had been
maintained and was still in perfect working order. The
ivory stop knobs were perfectly preserved, as were the lat-
ticework around the top of the organ, a music rack and a
lamp holder. My father's sister, who had accompanied my
parents on their trip, had played the organ and found it to
be remarkably well tuned. So was the bell, purchased long
ago for twenty-five dollars, used to call people to worship. I
couldn't resist pulling the rope several times. The clarion-
clear sound seemed to drift across the quiet landscape and
take its rest among those buried in the adjoining cemetery
dating back to 1905. The ensuing silence, devoid of noise
and distractions, seemed to beckon us to take up a conversation with the voice of our Creator and with those who are
the sources of inspiration.

Gratitude leaves a priceless imprint on our lives.

The role of my grandfather, as a preacher, began to envelope me as I surveyed the worship space. I gently ran my hands around the wooden spindles and across the communion rail where people had gathered to be nourished and strengthened for what lay ahead. I wondered what longings and troubles they brought with them as they came up the aisle bent upon getting closer to God. What spiritual blessings were poured into their laps and spilled over as an experience of gratitude? What was the content of their prayers of thanksgiving and the requests of their hearts?

The brown-varnished pulpit, a waist-high sturdy structure, included an elevated platform for a Bible. The front of the pulpit was tooled with spindles similar to those used for the communion rail. The varnished wainscoting and lightly tinted walls behind the pulpit dignified its presence and drew attention to its purpose.

The pulpit was situated near one of four tall clearglass windows, each capped by a sharply pointed arch. The light from one of them passed directly over the left shoulder of the preacher. I imagined the light drifting across the pages of scripture and lifting the words to be spoken by my grandfather. The light must have been cast brilliantly around him, for people recall him as a dramatic figure.

I could not resist making my way to the pulpit and taking my grandfather's place behind it. I fixed my hands on the pulpit with the authority of one preparing to preach. I wanted to get some sense of what it might have been like to look out on a congregation of probably twenty-five to thirty people, and bring the message from scripture that had been written to address the needs of generations to come. I tried to imagine what I might have said, knowing something of the geography and history of the people, to those in that time and place who came to hear the word of God. What passages from scripture, intended to fulfill God's noble purposes, prompted by the Spirit, spoken from the heart, might feed these often weary, yet resolutely faithful people? Scripture gives timeless testimony to another time and place, providing a seamless connection to our life's work. A building may be silent, but the voices that once populated it continue to speak to those who listen with their hearts and let what they hear sink into their souls. I am grateful for those moments when there is a deep sense of belonging to something I cannot touch.

That evening, despite all I had to be grateful for that day, I felt something was missing during our visit at the church. I could not put the feelings into words, but it seemed like a forlorn restlessness that beckoned me back to the church. The uneasiness persisted as we prepared to begin another day, and after talking it over with my wife, we decided to rearrange our schedule and return to the church. Later she said the entire trip would have been cast in shadow had we not returned. On the way, my wife said, "I think you should go inside alone and spend some time without any distractions." She would stay outside examining the tombstones. I was grateful for her sensitive appraisal of the situation and willingness to give me time on my own.

As we approached the church, I could see a woman sitting on the steps, and my heart sank. We were not going to be there alone. I saw the woman not as a person, but as an intrusion on an experience of silence and solitude. How could this happen? What in the world was she doing there? The questions coursed through my mind while I tried to absorb the disappointment. How could I be cordial when all I could feel was a lack of hospitality?

Gratitude blends a generous spirit with an expansive heart.

We got out of the car while she waited for us to come to her. She was wearing a simply cut, flowered dress, well-worn brown oxford shoes, and a white lace skullcap. She was not wearing makeup, and her pale skin revealed a person who seldom spent time out of doors. She seemed uneasy as we approached. We greeted her as we neared the steps where she was standing. She remained motionless and greeted us with an uncertain smile and a soft tentative voice. She told us she had heard the church bell peal the day before and that sound seemed to beckon her. I told her that I had rung the bell yesterday and was pleased to learn she had received it as an invitation to prayer. I asked her if she would like to come into the church and pray, as that was what I planned to do. Without hesitation, she accepted the offer, and, surprisingly, I was not upset she had done so. In a similar situation, I can imagine extending the invitation and then hoping it would not be accepted. My wife sensed this meeting was not accidental and thought to herself, "There is more here than meets the eye." She excused herself by saying, "You two go off to pray while I go off to read the stories in the cemetery."

Inside, we were greeted by six rows of high-backed wooden chairs and sat down directly across from one another on either side of the aisle. I felt peaceful with what had transpired during our brief exchange outside. I began trying to get in touch with the spirit of those who had prayed in the church during my grandfather's pastorate. She was not a distraction; in fact, her presence seemed to add something to the sacred connection we were both seeking. The silence was so pure I could detect the synchronicity of our breathing that seemed to evolve into a blessing. We both seemed to be inheriting the lessons left by those who came there before us. Maybe our prayers were an echo of those earlier worshippers. God preserves their memory in the hearts of those who come to honor them.

At some point, I could not resist turning toward her and thanking her for joining me. I said, "Although we have not spoken a word to each other, I feel our prayers speak of our common humanity." We had only just met one another in prayer, but I told her that I felt I knew her outside of this time. She turned her chair toward me, and a few tears gently traced a path down her face. She began to share her difficulties as a wife and mother in this lonely out-post, describing a life given over to physically repetitious, demanding, and exhausting duties without relief. Her life seemed devoid of appreciation and affirmation. She seemed embarrassed by these disclosures and began to apologize for being ungrateful for what she had. She invoked God as a generous giver and stable source of comfort in her life. She did not want to appear unappreciative for God's benevo-lence and for the comfort she received from prayer.

I could see she was gradually closing the door on what she had revealed, and I thanked her for letting me into her life. I told her I had come to the church to spend some time alone but that God had other plans; she had become an additional answer to my prayers as well as part of them. I was grateful, I told her, that she had put me in touch with the spirit I came to experience and that she was a gift I could only have imagined with my heart and soul. She stood up facing me, and we fell into an embrace that prob-ably lasted only thirty seconds, but seemed like an eternity. At that moment I knew the meaning of agape love. This was the unmerited way God loves when all the guards are let down and our vulnerabilities unite us as a simple anti-dote to our loneliness and our persistent restlessness for him. The missionary spirit of my grandfather was at work in the church, a place where strangers meet and learn they are one in the Spirit, one in the Lord.

Gratitude often follows unexpected events taken for what they are. Sometimes we have to be available to life and let it come to us, without trying to envision and plan for all the possibilities. At times we should risk uncertainty and open ourselves to potential discoveries.

For me, this most momentous experience started out as a terrible disappointment. Someone else was an obstacle to my plans. Instead, she redefined and completed them. I only needed to accommodate the trajectory for the unexpected for it to become a source of great joy and the fulfillment of my hopes. At times, the best things in life may happen when we least expect them. The core of gratitude includes instances of sheer delight when life surprises us.

Gratitude builds bridges between tranquility and surprise.

Gratitude is life-sustaining and can carry us through rough times. We can store away deposits of gratitude and draw upon them when our emotional bank account runs dry. We can remind ourselves that seldom will life be perfect. Gratitude can carry us through the less than satisfying and fulfilling times, when results fail to match expectations and the future looks less than promising.

Life is not meant to be a museum where we collect, preserve, and display the artifacts of living. Rather, we might live more fully if we take the perspective of artists, who know only the beginning and trust the experience to deliver the essence of an outcome. Such uncertainties may make us uncomfortable, but we really do not have as much control over the larger picture and details as we might like to believe. Perhaps we should be more accepting of risk and the possibilities it opens up to us.

Gratitude provides the thread to interweave hope and happiness.

REFLECTION TODAY

Life does not always deliver what we order, regardless of our well-conceived plans. We are seldom perfectly attuned to all the things going on around us, and we have to make adjustments and accommodations for the unanticipated and the unwelcome.

Recall a time when you believed you had meticulously put everything in place and felt assured everything would go according to plan. But beneath your well-planned future, there lurked some unforeseen circumstances that would squeeze the pleasure out of your plans. Yet, the pleasure of accepting and living with the unanticipated surpassed your original expectations. Life had a different agenda, and you benefited from its life-altering effects. How did gratitude become a blessing in disguise when you looked back upon this unanticipated happening? How has this experience prepared you to be more open to adventure and serendipity? How has gratitude been the forerunner of attitudes that have increased the likelihood of serendipitous events?

REFLECTION TOMORROW

Yesterday you dealt with a blessing in disguise, one that you did not initially welcome. At first disappointed, eventually you came to appreciate what was unplanned and unwelcome. The unanticipated included lessons you may not have learned any other way. Use gratitude to reflect on the experience. How did reconstructing the event make a difference in the way you felt about it?

CHAPTER 7
Passion

Gratitude daringly risks the future.

Every family seems to jump on and off a merry-go-round of annual events over the year. These events are eagerly anticipated and occasionally marked by high excitement. Gratitude works its way into the mix because each year everyone knows what to expect and how to prepare.

Every year our family attended a county fair or a local community celebration including a popular carnival. We gave our children each the purchase price for five rides, but our daughter at age six already knew her passion in life. She was not enamored of the glitz of wooden horses attached to a vertical pole. She wanted to mount and ride the real thing. She knew where to look for the pony ride as soon as she walked through the fair's gate. The ponies were always relegated to the fringes of the grounds, because ponies can be a little temperamental and obstinate, especially when surrounded by raucous activities. Thus, they were attached to horizontal poles stretching out from a center ring.

These ponies were not physically distinctive or attractive. They all shared common attributes; dappled, gloomy gray, with tangled manes, potbellies, and swaybacks that

nicely accommodated a black lackluster saddle. With droop-
ing ears and stooping heads, they appeared to be standing
on their last legs. They were hardly a match for their strik-
ingly colored wooden counterparts on the merry-go-round.
Little did this matter to our daughter. She used her imagination to create her own particulars and wove them into an
event of her own making.

The ponies, although indifferent to our daughter's
presence, did not discourage her from entering her circle
of delight. Entering this world depended upon two reliable sources of energy — the rider and the grandfatherly
assistant who lifted her onto the pony. Once mounted, our
daughter knew exactly what to do. She sat astride the pony
with the *regal* bearing of a princess, took the reins with
dignified aplomb, and eyed the scene with the loveliness of
an angel. The circle of her delight stood in stark contrast
to the one traced on the dusty earth by the slow gait of the
ponies.

The predictable path is a roundabout way of maintain-
ing an orderly path to nowhere. But for our daughter, this
was a place where the distance traveled hardly mattered,
even though the length of the ride varied by the size of the
circle, the number of ponies, the number of patrons, and the
heart of the owner. The circle pony ride became our girl's
world, where the real world provided an entry to her dreams.

In the pony fantasy world, where the small space is
framed by joy, and distance is the interval between rides
— time, space, and distance are meaningless points of reference. Life stands still as our daughter is enchanted by
having her dream realized. With a soulful gaze, she per-
sonifies pure innocence and ceaseless grace. Life does not
get any better than this. During the brief span of her ride,
she is transported into a perfect world, reflected in her
sparkling eyes.

Although she must eventually dismount, this is but a momentary interruption. Once returned to earth, she is back in line purchasing a second ticket. She makes the trip to this celestial sphere until she exhausts all her resources. Then, like a monk following prayer, she lifts her eyes in our direction and shares the blessing of God's handiwork. She knows the rapture and ecstasy of having been inside a perfect place. We are grateful bystanders who see how good life can be; we leave feeling transformed by the experience.

Gratitude lives simply and abundantly.

Now she is grown. I look back on these glorious moments and am reminded we are children of God and remain in his love. We are given brief custody of our children and are invited to participate in God's divine presence in their lives. We are meant to know something of the way God delights in us by seeing his love poured out in the innocence and joys of our children. Parenting is a solemn duty, an extension of God's reach and desire for our children to become the fulfillment of his love. We still observe her remarkable capacity to transform a simple event into breakthrough moments of passion and joy.

We all need a passion in our lives. With a passion, we empty ourselves of all life's distractions so we can seek the perfect place. It is a condition that invites us to make the most of right now. Sometimes we don't have to go anywhere or do anything; we just sit astride life and let life do its thing. There is something transcendent about life when it is suspended in time. It is a paradoxical moment when nothing and something are fused into a celestial relationship. This in-between condition is like riding a pony and believing this is the essence and nothing more.

Gratitude is often the forerunner of this condition. It provides reassurance, calms the spirit, and harnesses confidence. We are less inclined to harbor doubts and be tentative about tomorrow. We do not invest our energy in questioning our fears, recalling our failures, and revisiting our uncertainties. All we need is today and what now has to offer. We throw ourselves into what we believe is the best of who we are, leaving "should be" and "ought to do" for tomorrow. Today is the world of our own making. We are grateful for the day because it is a gift of twenty-four hours to be spent on what feeds our desire to make the most of what we have been given and to be something more than we have been. We adopt a healthy "what's next?" attitude.

Our daughter's todays gradually piled one upon the other. She arrived at the age when she wanted to replace the fella with ponies with the prized purchase of her own horse. This thrilling beginning was followed by many years of additional responsibility and pleasure. She no longer depended on a local celebration for her annual encounter with repeated joy. Instead, she crossed the road to enter a pasture where delight was a short distance away. She called "Drummer," and he would run to greet her. Both knew what awaited them, an apple and strokes of affection for one, and for the other the simple pleasure of sitting in a place where hopes are cherished and life locates moments of true happiness.

A neighbor girl had the same hopes, and arrangements were made to share the pasture. It was the beginning of a two-family enterprise in which two daughters knew their dads were subject to not-so-subtle persuasion. Our daughter got the best of the arrangement. The dad of her soon-to-be inseparable friend was a master of many trades. The girls were quick to seize upon his ability to make and fix things. Within a few months, before wind and cold and snow would make life less pleasant for the horses and more difficult for the girls, they commandeered both of us to construct a lean-to, eventually a building with two stalls, a tack room, and an enclosure to store one hundred bales of hay. He used his knowledge and ingenuity to locate a potential water source, sink a sand point to tap a water supply, and attach a pump for the girls to secure water. With all of these accommodations and a zest for placing their horses in the center of their lives, the girls made their way to the pasture almost every day. They seldom complained about the duties of feeding and caring for their animals.

My sixth-floor office at the university was strategically located for a privileged view of the girls' comings and goings. Riding a horse around barrels or galloping between both ends of the pasture replaced riding ponies in a circle. And there were leisurely walks where imagination was given enough space to play.

Eventually the pasture experiences were linked to other activities — parades and horseshow competitions — until going to college necessitated a tearful parting. Our daughter did not outgrow her devotion and affection for her horse, nor did she lack gratitude for being able to satisfy a desire.

A desire is simply a fanciful vision of nascent reality; passion is the energy that fuels and directs its realization. Passion was a centerpiece in our daughter's storied pilgrimage from little girl with hired ponies to young woman with her own horse. The pathway from a desire to reality is known to anyone who has lived inside a passion that refuses to give up.

We come to know passion as a force that has a pervading influence on our life. We do not waste energy on regrets that have little to teach us or on a future that offers little to recommend it. Yet our passions are fueled by reminders of our successes and the wisdom derived from our mistakes. We learn how to make wise expenditures of time and energy, how to size up possibilities. We are at once cautious and optimistic. We realize circumstances are often due to things we cannot anticipate or control. We strive to optimize success by paying attention to the past, but we do not let it make us indentured servants.

We take measured steps toward our destination, often using a mental yardstick to calculate the distance between where we are and where we plan to go. Yet, a yardstick is not calibrated to measure the distance between happiness and delight. The search for one puts the process in motion; the other tells us we have made a perfect choice.

Gratitude chooses wisely.

One's passions do not have to forever produce perfect outcomes. We do not always get exactly what we want. Our eagerness and enthusiasm may lack the intensity to establish a compelling purpose, produce a focused commitment, and harness well-directed behaviors. Adversity may make it difficult to maintain the original power of engagement and sustain a prolonged period of dedicated involvement. The flame of desire may flicker when it is not fueled by the cooperation of others similarly disposed and devoted to a cause. We may reach for the stars, but there are limits to how far we can stretch. Passion does not always get a hands-on confirmation of what it wants.

Passion can be fueled by where we have been as well as where we are going. Our daughter's wild anticipation of the next county fair was anchored in her memories of a joyous past. Although each of her experiences was not exactly the same, one doesn't need an exact replica of an experience to rekindle the excitement. Rather, passion is like the

snowflakes in a translucent winter globe, settled and waiting to be shaken up. Shake the globe and each flake floats
upward and then settles until roused again. It does not
occupy the same space each time it is brought to life.

Gratitude is both the father and mother of passion.
Paternally, gratitude looks beyond the present; it is expansive and protective. Maternally, gratitude looks inward; it
is settled, sanguine, and reassuring. This parental partnership sparks curiosity and nurtures creativity.

There is no end to passionate possibilities when gratitude is a bedrock attitude for building a life. We build on
the thankfulness of knowing we have the foresight and
stamina to search beyond our reach. Gratitude anticipates
good results when life is an open book. The story may be
of a small child holding reins in one hand and reaching
for whimsy with the other. The child sits in a saddle surrounded by endless possibilities. A passion is the simple
wonder of an angel come down from heaven to be a benedic-
tion and leave a parcel of spiritual joy.

All is right with the world when a little bit of heavenly bliss encircles imagination. Our daughter could live
in a sacred moment surrounded by the heavenly hosts, but
eventually she had to rejoin reality. A passion can only temporarily lift us to another level.

Gratitude forms buoyant connections between passion and perfection.

Desires often emerge from small and simple beginnings. Our daughter learned to wait a year between times
when the fella with the ponies showed up at the fair and
lifted her up to her sacred place. Something eternal wraps
this ephemeral moment with an indefinable essence. We do
not try to understand it, nor should we try to explain it. We

accept it as a gift. With her five tickets, our daughter was able to purchase a little slice of bliss. Paradoxically, gratitude is both the price we pay and what is returned to us — often a hundredfold.

Gratitude takes out a generous lease on life's pleasures.

REFLECTION TODAY

Passion may be thought of as a condition of the heart. Generally passion involves intense emotions that serve to ignite and direct one's choices and actions. Passion can be put in service of an activity or invested in the quest for a particular object. My daughter's passion for ponies is an example of passion aimed at securing the use of an object for a potentially satisfying experience. Gainful use of time on the ponies was the primary motive directing her actions.

Other passions are rooted in strong emotions sustained by deeply rooted values and are applied to various action-oriented priorities. The priorities often originate from earlier experiences of happiness. Passions fuel hope, which lead to a commitment and goal-directed behaviors. Zeal helps create a grand design, select appropriate strategies, order one's life, measure progress, and celebrate achievements.

My daughter's passion for ponies is now a collection of settled memories. Her passion for children and adults as a speech pathologist is no less satisfying — just otherwise directed.

Do you have a passion that you have channeled into a worthy goal, a passion whose absence would have created a vacuum in your life? How has the passion sustained and produced results that have been, and possibly continue to be, a source of joy and personal growth?

Name the object you were determined to use or the objective you resolutely set out to achieve.

Reflect upon and list the influences that contributed to the desire, boosted the drive, and prolonged your efforts.

How was gratitude instrumental in making your choice and sustaining your efforts?

How has gratitude itself been served because your passion was put in the service of a desired object and/or hoped-for outcome?

REFLECTION TOMORROW

Passion is a noun. We can make it a verb by actively putting ourselves into it. We can use our imagination to create a desire for something or grow a vision. We think positively to generate enthusiasm and decisively deploy the energy to produce behaviors and coordinated actions taking baby steps to achieve a goal.

Decide to make gratitude a centerpiece of your life. Become more mindful of its importance and deliberately look for silver linings in the daily events of your life. Be an advocate for gratitude's purpose and a practitioner of its merits.

What small steps can you take to get started, ones that will likely reinforce your early efforts to succeed?

What can you do to maintain a forceful and fruitful focus on gratitude as a staple in your life?

How can gratitude itself be a source of resolve and a reward for whatever good comes from your efforts?

CHAPTER 8
Misfortune

Gratitude blesses this day as a
gift to the one that will follow.

We often read newspaper and magazine accounts of people who have averted a tragedy. They are so grateful to be alive. They vow to devote their lives to saving others from suffering a similar fate and to turn their lives around. Life is no longer ordinary; everyday becomes a purpose chosen, a claim lived, and a realization of life offered and fulfilled. Life is not merely an endless day-to-day experience with a "come what may" attitude. When they set out to do something, they do not permit distractions to tempt them to do otherwise. They find themselves anchored to a willful decision. They know what they want to do and learn what it takes to do it. They seem undaunted by hardship or setbacks. They emphasize the positive and dismiss the negative, embracing every success with gratitude. Gratitude acts like a catalyst for action. It fortifies their beliefs that nothing else really matters and what matters most is going about living the ideal they espouse.

When I was about twelve, I finally thought I was ready to pass the test to swim in the deep end of the municipal pool. Many kids my age had already learned how to swim the distance required to be admitted to the deep end of the pool. The decision had to be tested under the watchful eye of a lifeguard. He ruled over a not-so-vast domain, but it was one in which I would gladly be a willing subject. He was bound by duty, I by rules to demonstrate my ability to enter the kingdom. My decision would be an assault on my fear and a struggle to swim above the surface of my doubts. Each stroke would be a test of my courage and an effort to preserve my pride. The lifeguard nodded and smiled encouragingly. He may have seen the apprehension in my eyes and the mental strain mirrored in a tense body. My decision was not without frightful reservations.

I was not comfortable in the water and was not a very proficient swimmer. I was hesitant to take a chance and filled with self-doubts and apprehension. I surveyed the situation. The distance was once around the area that enclosed ten feet of water. There would be no standing on the bottom if I tired. A lot was at stake, but I was tired of just treading the water of my fears. Nudged somewhat by pride, I was prompted even more by my desire to swim with my friends who had already mastered the challenge I was about to undertake. Their urgings had brought me to this day. Their reassurance and confidence would buoy me up. They would be both the strength and encouragement I needed. I was grateful to have friends who believed in me, saw past my fears, and looked toward the time we could enjoy one another's company with the "big kids."

Gratitude reassures us we are more than we have proven.

As a novice swimmer, the challenge loomed large. I looked at the lifeguard enthroned high above the edge of the pool before I made my entry. There was nothing to suggest he didn't believe I was ready and able. I dove into the pool and began an assault on my fears and limitations. I swam about three-quarters around the perimeter of the pool before I sensed I was in trouble. I struggled to keep my head above the water and my energy had been depleted. My arms felt like pudding. I seemed to be repeatedly stroking the same dense space below me. My legs drooped like grapes on a vine. Only sheer determination, laced with fear of going under, kept me afloat. In retrospect, I suspect the lifeguard knew I was in trouble but was waiting to see if I would recover. I knew what it was like to be oxygen deficient. With a few lengths remaining, a boy, unaware of my presence and predicament, dove off the high board. As he entered the water, his feet clipped my body and I lost the small amount of breath my lungs were conserving to win my battle with fatigue. As I struggled to stay on top of the water, fear began to get the best of what was left of me. It gripped my mind and wrung out what little energy remained. I began to struggle below the surface. The soul does serve as a screen and during a few fleeting moments projects the passing of a lifetime.

All at once, I felt a pair of hands clutch my waist. The lifeguard tucked my exhaustion under his strong arms and thrust me head first through the water's surface. I was gasping for air as my head broke through the darkness into the light above me. The lifeguard held me aloft. As we bobbed in the water, his words were reassuring. I knew I was in safe hands. I did not have time to be embarrassed or humiliated. Life is too precious to waste part of it by refusing to accept our limitations and vulnerability. I was grateful to be alive. Together, we had averted a tragedy.

Gratitude clutches us with life-bearing hands in times of disaster.

Unlike persons who have struggled to survive a near-death experience, I was not inspired or disposed to take up a life-long cause. At twelve years of age, distant goals were hardly a developmental possibility. My gratitude was probably short-lived. Adolescence is rarely a time when one dwells on the past and draws upon it to set one's course. There is so much immediacy bidding for one's attention. The past is a few days long and the future is only the day after tomorrow. Getting on with life is doing what comes naturally. Life has not yet become a quest because there is so much more to learn. Life is more like an unfettered journey.

As we get older, a close brush with death is much more significant. We pay more attention to death when each year points us in this direction. With additional years of maturity, the inevitable loss of our ability to do things we formerly did with ease, our dependence on others to help us through various setbacks, and our reading of obituaries as a matter of practice make us more aware of our vulnerabilities. We catch glimpses of our mortality. Death sometimes stops us in our tracks.

I attend many wakes, funerals, and memorial services. They open doors to gratitude as the deceased reminds us who they were and who we are. We use the narrative of the deceased's life to write an obituary, visit with the family, prepare a eulogy, and offer personal remarks at a wake or memorial service. We retrace our history and remember the situations that pleasingly and uniquely joined us one to another. Recalling the good times and special places give us pause to be wonderfully, mindfully, and humbly grateful. We reflect on the content of that life and recount the ways the deceased has enriched and ennobled us. Testimonials extol exceptional qualities, applaud prized talents, and praise thoughtful deeds, gestures, and practices. We more fully appreciate the enormity of their influence, the extent and scope of their activities, and the privileged impact of their generosity. They have built a bridge between heaven and earth. We cross over each time we take communion in remembrance of them.

These are the "I will never forget" bonding experiences anchored in gratitude. They are the resurrection and life-everlasting remembrances that prompt us to emulate what we have learned and appreciate. There are also the "I regrets," the things we should have said and done that would have required so little effort, yet would have meant so much. They serve to make us more intent upon elevating their goodness while evaluating our own. We are more mindful of pathways to goodness and lifelines to happiness. Gratitude serves as an antidote to our forgetfulness to appreciate and reminds us of the simple ways we can be more loving of each other. Gratitude is like a linchpin that connects us to life and death experiences.

I wonder what we would be like if we used our losses, particularly of loved ones, to become more attentive and appreciative of those who transport us to choice places and shower us with good times. We might use gratitude as a template to revisit the situations and events of each day. The template would help us identify the people who, by virtue of their proclivities and actions, contributed something worthwhile and noteworthy during our day. We would then pinpoint and appreciate some of the qualities and behaviors that warrant prayerful recognition in our hearts and, on occasion, some tangible expression of gratitude.

I believe this practice could become a gratitude-inspiring and gratitude-enabling activity. It would produce gratitude-forming attitudes and gratitude-affirming practices. We might approach life with a more approving attitude and be more prone to see the positive side of a person and event. We might be more hospitable to ourselves, more forgiving of our mistakes, less likely to harbor grievances and the unintended trespasses of others. Life would be more agreeable because gratitude is a virtue that feeds and transforms all others. Taking samples of goodness provides us with the material to grow ourselves into more upright and grateful people. Our gratitude may not inspire a cause nor set our hearts and souls afire. But gratitude does awaken us to our potential for making something happen that stirs and sustains its presence elsewhere.

Gratitude supplies us with multiple perspectives.

I now have the longevity to look back with this kind of gratitude. With the clarity of time as my witness, I can now collect and consider instances wherein gratitude beckoned for my attention. It gradually became an essential ingredient in my recipe for living. Life-long encounters with gratitude have been tucked in and folded over into the corners of life. Like blankets, gratitude can be a source of warmth and comfort.

I came to realize gratitude often lifts the fog that casts a shadow on the future. We often have to climb the mountain to see beyond the dailiness of our lives. We can become so encumbered by what is right in front of us that we lack a vision of what can be. When we see and feel anew, life is

more like an open door than a dead-end road. Life is trans-
figured — a resurrection experience. We come down from
the mountain and take up where we left off. However, the
experience will have made a claim on our lives. We will
never be the same nor would we want to be.

Gratitude serves as a lifeline to the future.

Gratitude is a good way to redraw the boundaries of
life and strike out for territory yet to be explored. Gratitude
can be the spark and the tinder that keeps our love of life
burning. We are indeed fortunate when gratitude is an
ever-present companion and reminder of our blessings.
Sometimes it takes a brush with death to awaken us to a
powerful and instinctive desire to change. We don't want to
be scared to death but sometimes we need to be shaken free
of entrenched habits in our thinking and doing. Only when
we are set free of fixed patterns of behavior can we redirect
our resources and put them in the service of something better. Habits are formed and maintained by repetitive ways of
seeing and doing. They often outlast their usefulness. Only
a life-and-death encounter may get them to yield to more
helpful and effective ways of behaving. Only then can one
break away from what is detrimental to begin living the
possibilities and investing in the future.

Most of us will not be rescued from the edge of death.
We are more likely to experience death in small doses. We
will swim in troubled water but will manage to stay afloat.
More often, trouble comes to us from the circumstances of
our lives. We just get in the way of living as we like, and
someone or something refuses to cooperate. We may be
content to stay at the shallow end of the pool — where it is
refreshing and there are plenty of opportunities for having

a good time — until someone gets the idea a better time can be had elsewhere. In my case, the elsewhere could not be claimed as a place to have this better time without facing what was a troubling reality: I could not be included — unless I grew myself into the required behaviors. I had to decide whether being included warranted the risk.

Gratitude mobilizes our inner resources.

Much of life involves making decisions about being included. We want to be taken into account and deemed worthy to be part of what is going on around us. We often like to be right in the center of things. We want to be totally engaged when everyone else is having fun. Our troubles seem to fade away when we make friends with amusement and playfulness. We can take ourselves too seriously when learning how to swim and can risk too much before we are ready. We are grateful when we accurately measure the risks, ensure ourselves against a loss in self-esteem, and cover our bets by preparing to gamble with no more than we have to lose. Someone may rescue us when we misjudge the situation or ourselves, but we do not count on it. Most will not have a lifeguard to rescue them from death-dealing events or dangerous choices. However, in less dramatic and possibly unrecognized ways, we have been rescued from hundreds, even thousands, of dangerous situations unbeknownst to us.

Gratitude succeeds although success seemed unlikely.

I was rescued from death when I was twelve years old. Sixty years later I am recalling and writing about this experience. Maybe this book is in some ways rooted in that experience. I was thrust out of the water and plunged into an additional sixty fruitful and fulfilling years. Possibly I have taken on this crusade on behalf of gratitude because it did not become a touchstone and mainstay much earlier in my life. I absolve myself by believing I was too young to understand and appreciate the full impact of a near-death experience and its life-long ramifications. I certainly wasn't ready to become a life-long advocate for water safety, a proponent for teaching everyone to swim. However, I can see how there would have been far-reaching benefits of being able to conceive of the multiple meanings of gratitude and discover its manifestations during the intervening years of my life. This book is a culmination in some ways of this realization. Every consequence does not evoke a cause. But every cause does help others to take it up and claim it as their own. To live gratitude can be a lightning rod for some and an intravenous feeding for others.

Gratitude changes the plot line of our lives.

Life is not confined to the small areas of a municipal swimming pool. There isn't always someone sitting in a lofty position prepared to pull us out when we go under. Yet, to live fully, we have to take our chances. There will always be risks when we want to be included with those who have already proven themselves. We have to ask ourselves if what they did to be approved is worthy of our commitment. Unfortunately, the hazards of living are greater when we enter the deeper waters that require boldness and courage. However, we do not need a single death-defying experience to look at life through the lens of our rich resources and to see places where we can make and be a difference. We do not need to be a hero for a cause to demonstrate the power of thankfulness in our lives. We only need recognize the preciousness of life and varied ways it can be invested on behalf of others.

We will all have several scrapes with potential death-dealing events and the consequences. Each can make a contribution to a gratitude-affirming outlook and to gratitude-oriented choices and behaviors. The setbacks we experience can be used to help others rebound from their own setbacks. There is the daily discovery of instances wherein gratitude makes us available to some and provides the power to electrify life and lift up others. In many ways life and death are not very far apart. The beginning and end of each day can be profitably used to take an inventory of our gratefulness for each condition. We can learn to be thankful for what has been learned in our giving and receiving. Our handiwork and hardships can bear fruit when we approach them with gratitude and look for the blessings that warrant this attitude of gratitude. Life is always indebted to gratitude for life itself depends upon it.

Gratitude regards a setback as a mere point in time.

REFLECTION TODAY

Many of the "in my day" stories include elements of mistakes and misfortune. They are the mishap stories we exchange when others are bent upon telling theirs. Not infrequently our stories may seem to be told as "one-upmanship" accounts of our lives. We do not intend it to diminish the significance of another's experience or lessen the importance of the lessons they learned from the experience. Our story is an attempt at empathy; it is intended to say, "I can understand what you are saying, and I can relate to what you have gone through. I have been there and know what it is like." Our story can be misconstrued to be one-upmanship although this is seldom the intent. We just want the story to be sufficiently, emotionally compelling to indicate misfortune is a common denominator, a demonstrable source of solidarity. The exchanges offer potentially useful ways to deal with the hard knocks life delivers regardless of who we are and what we do.

Recall one of your misfortune stories, a time when life dealt a severe blow to your physical, social, economic, or spiritual well-being. You were struck a blow below the belt, lost your breath, and were temporarily knocked you off your feet. You had to stand up, brush yourself off, and get on with life. What happened that you were unprepared to deal with? What was most shocking or devastating about this event/situation and/or change in the way you viewed yourself and/or your connection to life? What were your initial attempts to deal with this marked change in yourself and/or the circumstances of your life? Who or what was available to you as you began your assault on this "misfortune" mountain? What did they supply that helped you climb up and down? What did you learn about yourself, others, and life that has become an essential part of who you are and what you strive to be? How has your experience helped you use misfortune, your response to it, and others' participation in your response to be formed in gratitude and to use gratitude to affect the lives of others?

REFLECTION TOMORROW

Everyone can look back upon misfortune and make a case for its benefits. In retrospect, we might even be grateful for it. We cannot imagine valuing who we are, what we have done, and what we currently are doing in the absence of some ordeals. Yet, we generally do not deliberately choose adversity for the potentially useful lessons it might teach us. Despite our tendency to avoid accidents, or lessen their effects, we do occasionally choose adversity and its companion, discipline, because we believe it can teach us something we cannot learn any other way.

Recall an ordeal you have deliberately chosen for its potentially life-giving lessons and/or challenging requirements. Or select an ordeal that would require a commitment you feel unprepared to make. This ordeal would require "walking the walk." It is intended to express a deeply held value and will require you to live without the benefit of comforts and conveniences you prize. You would be confronted with a stark reality you can only imagine. How do thoughts of gratitude serve as a source of inspiration, encouragement, and strength as you contemplate making friends with a potentially calamitous event and then choosing it despite your doubts and fears? Or in the second instance, how might gratitude help you imagine and anticipate the gratitude of others and your own gratitude for taking a risk to live boldly and courageously? How might gratitude help overcome your resistance and fears and compensate you for your decision to be more than you think you can be?

CHAPTER 9

Kindness and Consideration

*Gratitude treasures both ends
of life and all days in between.*

Family vacations offer fresh possibilities for having fun. Vacations lift us out of the ordinary and whet our appetites for adventure. Two years before I completed my doctorate at Indiana University, I promised my wife and our children that we would celebrate this accomplishment and honor their contributions to it by doing something very special. The question, "What do you want to do, and where do you want to go to do it?" produced a spontaneous response: "Disneyland."

For my family, the adventure began in our imagination and gradually evolved into all kinds of mind-boggling preparations. We acquired the tools and practices of consumer consultants and human resource personnel. We decided we would try to conserve our resources en route so we could be mindless spendthrifts upon our arrival. We soon knew what we needed to do — doing it became a collaborative enterprise with exciting results.

Disneyland was the final destination. This was to be an adventure including many other venues along the way. We quizzed people who had made this trip and had discovered interesting places to visit and things to do. We followed these suggestions with letters requesting pamphlets and brochures. Excitement in the household mounted when our mailbox supplied another possibility. We entertained ourselves by pouring over the materials, comparing and contrasting possibilities, pinpointing locations on maps collected at our local filling stations, and making a list of tentative choices. We studied the appeal and features, evaluating the benefits of each choice. This was hands-on education and the lessons gradually produced a list of tentative choices. Agreements and priorities began to emerge as we narrowed the choices and planned the stopping points along the way, resulting in a daily itinerary. We felt ready to deal with unforeseen problems and chance opportunities. Anticipation mounted as we crossed off days to our departure on the calendar.

My wife and I decided to put structure on our itinerary to accommodate our children's ages — seven, eight, and ten. We scheduled our departures so the children would have to be awakened and would then readily fall asleep in the car. A time for breakfast and the distance to the first vacation site would determine the actual departure times. This provision and many car games — purchased and contrived — diminished backseat squabbles and inquiries about when we would get there. The children easily adapted to this routine and other scheduled activities throughout the day.

Gratitude often follows an orderly unfolding of plans.

We greatly underestimated just how extraordinary our trip would be and how serendipitous events would produce surprising results. Our first remarkable road trip experience occurred when we arrived at a spectacular panoramic view of a colorful valley. I knew about this off-the-road scenic viewing spot because I had been there several years earlier. When we reached the area, I was excited that my reaction lived up to my memory. The thrill was magnified because what I had previously spoken about could now be shared with the family. The scene laid before us was regal and magical.

The viewing area was atop a steep cliff, and large rocks, intended to be a warning and a safety measure, surrounded the perimeter of the parking area. Because I was so excited to share the scenic beauty, I drove too far forward, scraping the undercarriage of the car over the top edge of one of the rocks. The rock appeared to have punctured the radiator, causing a substantial deposit of liquid to pour on the ground. Instantly alarm and apprehension replaced thrill and happiness. How quickly one's view and experience of the world can change.

Shortly after I surveyed the damage to our car, another car pulled up along side of us. The driver calmly asked what had happened while he sized up the situation and quietly noted the disheartened look on my face. He examined the damage as I told him what had happened, but he was immediately reassuring. He said the radiator itself was not damaged but that a drain cap was dislodged and would need to be replaced. He spoke with the authority of someone who knew precisely what needed to be done, and he also volunteered to take me to a nearby town and give repair instructions to the garage mechanic. His confident

assessment of the situation was matched by kindly reassurance. Sometimes we can be rescued without doing anything
but standing by and waiting for someone who knows the
territory.

I wondered why, in addition to being so knowledgeable and proficient, he was so marvelously accommodating.
As it turned out, he operated a radiator repair service in
Davenport, Iowa. Later, I pondered the probability of someone with his expertise appearing just when we needed him.
But for now, I was grateful. He was foremost a fellow Iowan
doing what Iowans do. My family had many times received
as well as offered Iowa hospitality so we were not amazed
to have been rescued. This was but another instance of
what we had come to expect from our statewide soul mates:
a tradition of neighborliness. We don't really see a problem;
we see a person who needs help. It is simply the thing to do.

We've told this story on many occasions, and typically
people cannot resist offering an explanation. Coincidence is
often offered as the source of our "good fortune." Some said it
was an unlikely convergence of our dilemma and an appropriate solution. Good luck, not totally unlike good fortune,
is also a favored explanation. Luck defies predictability and
refuses to bow before uncertainty. Some listeners suggested
divine intervention as an answer to our prayers.

Gratitude sweeps us off our feet by unexpected accommodations.

The divine is a spiritually appealing explanation for
those who believe in a divine interest in our daily affairs.
This response reveals our seamless bond with the sacred.
We apprehend a divine connection that is not merely based
on coincidences; we envision a God who makes provisions
for playfulness and a spirit of adventure in the universe,

who allows us to participate in recreating the world through our imagination and transformative experiences. God welcomes the opportunity to make himself present in unlikely places and at unexpected times.

Our distress and exasperation during the valley trip served as an invitation for God to rouse and amaze us. He must take delight in shaking us free of our certainty and, by his grace, helping us use adversity as one condition for growth. And when explanations do not suffice, we accept that we have no ready answers for some questions. We can talk about coincidence, but somehow we sense there is more than meets the eye. Why God bothers with us, with a universe to mind, is part of the mystery. We can only try to understand and be grateful that he has not and will not abandon us. Rather, God does transfigure us.

Surprises lurked around the corner during our five-day trip from Iowa to California. While we had already experienced one mishap, hardship had been a stranger until we tried to prepare our first meal with our new Coleman stove, which for some reason did not heat liquids. Fortunately, another camper explained to us that we had left out one critical step. We were saved by meeting just the right person at the same site, at the same time, someone who provided exactly the information we needed. Gratitude often follows a convergence of seemingly accidental events that then miraculously set everything right. We sometimes stand in awe of the simplicity with which life greets us and wonder why the obvious is so difficult to discover.

Gratitude may follow small expenditures of mindfulness and effort.

On our trip we learned how some surprises are subject to modest man-made interventions. In our case, the unexpected was moderated by careful planning; we had the kind benefit of my brother's prior experience at Disneyland. We wanted to fully enjoy its wonders without compromising our ability to protect ourselves in a new and possibly overwhelming environment.

My brother, an elementary school principal who had taken children to Disneyland on many occasions, knew from his experience which rides were the most popular by the length of the lines and wait time. He advised us to be at the gate when the park opened and helped us maximize our two days at Disneyland with a prioritized list of venues and a map of their locations. Like a real estate agent, "location, location, location" became a prized piece of information. With his recommendations and discount tickets in hand, we set out to test his experience and our endurance.

On our first day, we went immediately to the first venue on the list and were among the first groups to enter. By midmorning, we had visited most of our priority attractions. Other than our first and second choice, we did have to wait in line, but never for more than thirty minutes. We put the remaining venues that required longer wait times at the top of the list for our second day. We were astonished at how accurately my brother had planned our two days.

Gratitude often begins
with who you know.

Standing in line gave us an opportunity to reflect on the kindness and consideration we'd been shown and to compare our strategy with that of others. We were surprised to learn most people relied upon the expressed interests of their children and posted estimates of wait times. We were thankful to have had "inside information" and a two-day window for exercising our options. Taking the guesswork out of an experience sometimes maximizes gratitude. Although, in the case of Disneyland, we had also heard plenty of stories about the importance of patience, tolerance, and endurance, we were fortunate these virtues were not required — excessively!

We can all recount experiences when consideration and kindness spared us the disagreeable effects of adversity. In this case my brother spared us the aggravation and restlessness of standing in long lines and making disappointing choices.

Gratitude celebrates gifts wrapped
in the experience of others.

Vacations require high energy but typically provide little control. Not everything occurs like clockwork or according to some well-conceived and executed plan. However, kindness and consideration eased our way and allowed greater happiness during the trip. We are fortunate when others extend the benefits of these attributes to us. As a family, we sensed the power of gratitude when consideration and kindness became forerunners of joy.

In addition to doing what we wanted to do together, our vacation became a way for us to bond as a family. Each day's activities fostered acts of helpfulness. Like the holding power of glue, kindness can also bind people together. Once applied to life, kindness withstands all the elements of disagreeableness that would undermine it.

Consideration is the reward we get when we take a vacation from everyday selfishness and put others' happiness before our own. It's not necessary to go to Disneyland to be invested in consideration. Consideration is a thoughtful investment we make in ourselves and a service rendered on behalf of others.

On our trip we were prepared to receive consideration and kindness. We put ourselves in harm's way when we risked leaving the predictability and stability of our comfortable life. But we also put ourselves on a pathway toward happiness by taking a chance on adventure and believing we would be rescued from misfortune. Consideration and kindness became mainstays in our lives and hallmarks of our experience with others. What we were given, we could then offer. We are doing what comes naturally when our lives are rooted in kindness and consideration.

We often discover gratitude by becoming considerate and kind. It is as if we are circuitry, looking for a pathway to complete us. We want to connect with life, to feel its power, and distribute its possibilities. When emboldened with gratitude, we want to make a difference. It is an energy that can be put in the service of consideration and kindness.

Our vacation story also showed me that consideration and kindness are a combination of aptitude and attitude. When a total stranger helped us with our radiator trouble, he immediately knew what was wrong and what needed to be done. Simply knowing would have been useless to us, but by applying his consideration and kindness, he made a difference. We benefited from his aptitude for knowing and doing and his attitude of being sensitive to our plight. The combination of aptitude and attitude became springboards for action. I was enormously grateful that he knew what to do and did it without any reciprocal expectations.

The kindness and consideration shown to us during that experience have not been lost when I've encountered the misfortune of others. Although the situations were not identical, I have had opportunities to help others many times. I, too, have been the stranger who knew something and could do something; I have been gratitude at work. I know its power to change an outlook and an outcome. We are no strangers to gratitude when we use what we have been given to help others who encounter misfortune. Consideration and kindness are accommodations we offer others to help temper the effects of adversity or prepare others to make the most of opportunity.

We grow in gratitude through small acts of kindness and consideration, gradually becoming a person who is defined by these qualities. Gratitude becomes a way of living life. We make ourselves available to the conditions in life that nurture it. We are willing to give the pleasure of it away to those who need a lift. The pleasure is multiplied by observing its capacity to nurture.

Gratitude places no limits on its patience and endurance.

REFLECTION TODAY

Consideration and kindness can be catalysts for richer experiences of gratitude.

Gratitude should be in plentiful supply in our culture where most have more than they need. Yet it seems that in our culture of excess consumption, where people aspire to have more than they need and are discontented when they do not have all they want, we have actually diminished the likelihood that gratitude will be a moving force in the service of the marginalized and disenfranchised. We are more likely to share the benefits of what we have been given when kindness and consideration supplant our preoccupation with ourselves. It is easier to be a giver when we regard all we have as gifts rather than as something we are entitled to.

Identify an instance when kindness and consideration were prime movers in your decision to help someone in need. What was it that prompted you to entertain these virtues? How did gratitude set your decision in motion and produced behaviors of kindness and consideration? How did the response of the recipients of your kindness and consideration increase or decrease the likelihood of your repeating this behavior in the future?

REFLECTION TOMORROW

Identify a time when you were treated with kindness and consideration. Compare your experience with the one you thought about yesterday. What were some of the differences and similarities between being the giver and the receiver? What do you better understand about the importance of gratitude in forming these two virtues? In what ways do you feel better disposed and better equipped to be a kind and considerate person after reflecting on the importance of gratitude as an incentive to practice these qualities in all meaningful relationships?

CHAPTER 10

Weather

*Gratitude welcomes and
moderates extremes.*

I live in the Midwest, where our stories are wrapped with appreciation for each season of the year. Spring, summer, fall, and winter take up residence in Iowa during each twelve-month cycle. We use a calendar to anticipate their arrivals and departures, but they are not subject to these arbitrary boundaries. Each season has its own form of presentation, spellbinding characteristics, and unique ways of heralding its coming in and going out. We learn to be alert and adapt to the elements of each season.

Iowans pay particular attention to such nuances because each season frames our thinking, feelings, and activities. Weather provides a common frame of reference for our conversations. Each season has its devotees, but we are bound together by spring and summer. Because we are an agricultural state, these two seasons influence our economic prosperity. Thus, we keep tabs on temperature and precipitation and their effects on a bountiful harvest. We value each season for its richness. Gratitude knows and appreciates the contribution each season makes to our livelihood and well-being. Despite the wonderful ways seasons transform the landscape of our lives, there is a downside to summers, especially in July.

Heat and humidity are burdensome mainstays of July's thirty-one days. We are put on notice when rising temperatures, conspiring with moisture drawn from the earth and sky, leave deposits of sweat coursing across our bodies. Most days create double-barreled misery that causes us to hide behind awnings, shades, and blinds. Aside from golfers, who seem to be oblivious to these oppressive conditions, most people stay inside. Yet these two disagreeable conditions, along with additional moisture, produce the perfect conditions for growing corn. We grow millions of bushels of corn in Iowa. Heat and humidity increase the growth and yield. Some say when heat and humidity are at their apex, one can actually stand in a cornfield at night and hear the corn growing. We celebrate corn that is knee-high by the Fourth of July.

Unlike the rest of the population, farmers seldom complain about heat and humidity. My mother, who detested heat and humidity, was a spokesperson for the rest of us. To her, heat and humidity were two unwelcome roomers joining our family during the summer months. They seized each day and took the pleasure out of living, spreading discomfort with their persistent presence. My mother was raised in a modest-sized house in a family of fourteen children; she might have been expected to deal easily with two new arrivals. Not the case with this pair.

As the summer wore on, heat and humidity became unbearable tenants. The mere mention of them elevated her discomfort and multiplied her complaints. She just didn't have enough stamina or patience to resist the effects of these interlopers. I believe my mother tried to be uncomplaining, but the conditions were difficult for her to ignore as she labored throughout the day. She may have been more severely afflicted because she was a high-energy, intensely engaged person, someone who did everything quickly and seldom paused to rest. Yet even chores that permitted her to stand still, such as doing dishes and ironing clothes, were heat-generating activities. She insisted on ironing all of our clothing; it was not uncommon for her to stand over an ironing board a couple of hours every evening. She never complained about the discomfort of performing these duties. She was doing what mothers do to raise a family, and I think she wanted our appearance each day to reflect those values.

I grew up observing my mother's discomfort and listening to her complaints. My mother used the date I was born, July 1, 1934, as the supreme example of a horrible and barely livable summer. That summer became her yardstick to measure the intensity of heat and humidity when we lived in St. Louis, not a congenial location for someone with her disposition.

As the story goes, and I remember it well, it would rain for about sixty minutes between the hours of 6 and 8 a.m. Then the clouds would scatter in a matter of minutes, and the sun would mercilessly beat down on the sidewalks and pavement. One could almost see, definitely feel, the steam rising as a cloud of vapor. A mass of tiny droplets would form on my mother's forehead and trickle down the side of her face. Before long, she was soaked in perspiration. Although my mother never made good on her claim, she insisted she could fry an egg on the sidewalk. The mere mention of St. Louis would help her selectively recall her long-standing protestations about our three summers there.

My father seldom broke a sweat during the summer. He seemed to be exempt from the discomforts of heat and humidity. Maybe he had built some kind of heat immunity while daily attending the contents of bakery ovens. Maybe his belief in mind over matter also spared him my mother's affliction. However, he was sympathetic to my mother's discomfort and distress. He listened to her misery-laden descriptions and became keenly attuned to the slight variations in the ways the heat and humidity affected her life. He realized that absent these conditions, my mother had a mild-mannered, pleasant, congenial temperament.

One summer my father purchased several oscillating fans and gave my mother custody of them. She became almost obsessed with maximizing the benefits of these devices, strategically locating them throughout the house during the day. The spinning fan blades created a breeze that seemed to push aside the heat and humidity. Actually the breeze transferred the sweat from our bodies to the already damp air around us. We dripped less; the air soaked up more. The outcome of the battle depended on the proper number and placement of fans. Although the fans could provide only temporary relief, at least my mother was shaping the situation more to our liking.

*Gratitude evolves within
small increments of progress.*

At night, my mother would strategically locate the fans in the bedrooms, with each fan's head tipped slightly toward the ceiling. All night, the breeze spread across our beds, supplying some welcome relief. There was something refreshing about the movement of air below, around, and above us. We knew the retreat during one cycle of the fan would be followed by an advancing column of air thereafter. The rhythmic movement of air changed the night from an unpleasant condition to one more to our liking.

Gratitude provides relief from objectionable situations.

In an ironic twist, in my mother's later years when she resided in a care center, she dressed much the same regardless of the season. I would make sure she wore a sweater when I took her out for lunch or for a leisurely ride in our air-conditioned car. When she napped, she would willingly curl up in the blankets without complaint.

My mother lived to be 94 years of age and was generally alert and interested in what it was like outside. She particularly liked to talk about changes during the four seasons of the year, describing her preference for spring and fall. Going outside in a wheelchair was a welcomed invitation for her to talk about the weather. As we left the building, she cheerfully greeted others with an elevated spirit of friendliness. Once outside she would perk up and take deep breaths of freedom. As we wandered around the adjoining neighborhood, her conversation would include references to the distinctive features of the weather of each season and her preferred activities. Spring was her favorite season providing relief from the dark, dreary days of winter. It was full of anticipation and surprise. She liked to reminisce and give an accounting of the gradual evolution of life everywhere. Seeing the first robin returning from a vacation down south was a particularly exuberating event. For those who arrived too early she would become a caretaker, replacing scarce worms and insects with peanut butter spread on bread, blueberries, and slices of apple. Occasionally a flock of twelve to fifteen robins would congregate and clamor about in the area she used as a feeding station.

Spring, pregnant with possibilities, witnesses new life emerging everywhere. Buds burst forth from growth left idle during the winter months. Crocuses are awakened from a long winter's nap; tulips shoot up, face the sun, and dance in the breeze. In her younger days, my mother would assist nature by raking leaves from her flowerbeds and garden plot. When the soil warmed, she would make her annual trip to the grocery store to purchase seed packets located on a spinning rack just inside the front door. The brightly illustrated packets tempted her to expand her inventory and test her ambition. Then, she would plant flower and vegetable seeds supplying the earth with additional items to grow.

She could not resist planting patches of annuals among her perennials. She wanted to create a cavalcade of color around the house and yard. The flowers were a welcoming presence at the front and back entrances of her house. With birds for company, she would weed, hoe, deadhead flowers, and water plantings. She also planted a small vegetable garden. I think she imagined the contents of the seed package would duplicate the stunning pictures on the outside. She would be thrilled to pull the bright orange carrots and deep red radishes from the dark soil. She dreamed of hills of potatoes to be unearthed like buried treasure, and succulent tomatoes that would yield tangy pleasure surpassing anything purchased at the grocery store. Spring was an awe-inspired, transformative experience. As spring gave way to summer, my mother had to deal with the burdens of heat and humidity. Thus, she rose early and fortified herself with a slice of whole-wheat toast slathered with homemade strawberry preserves and a cup of strong coffee before tackling chores like a soldier doing KP.

Gratitude flourishes in the spring when awe and wonder teach us the mystery of life unfolding. Spring radiates in all of life and the glow spills over into our hearts. Spring made everything ready for summer, whose fruitfulness was not lost on my mother. Abundance from her garden and thriving flowerbeds were blessings of the season, but they could not offset summer's brutal heat and drag-me-down humidity. Life was a waiting game between spring and fall. She could hardly wait for summer to be replaced by crisp, cool autumn days when she liked to take a slice of generously buttered toast and a cup of coffee outside to watch moisture evaporate and rise from dew sparkling in the sunlight. She experienced a resurgence of energy as the sun now brightened her day.

Every day contributed something to fall's spectacular beauty. Trees burst into a canopy of dazzling color. On a still day leaves drop from the trees in a hush, and settle to the ground where they gradually weave a multi-colored blanket around the tree's trunk. On other days, branches sway in the wind, creating a symphony of sounds with leaves performing a variety of dance steps. The wind lifts and sends leaves swirling through the air like little propellers. As the temperature falls and winds increase, large clusters of leaves descend like clouds, scatter, and come to rest in bushes and snuggle in crevices. Near the end of the life-and-death cycle, a slight breeze is sufficient to release the remaining leaves tenuously clinging to the tips of branches. After an overnight frost, an entire tree may dramatically drop its leaves all at once when touched by the morning sun.

Gratitude gradually creeps into our awareness when fall builds itself into a symphony of color, orchestrating a performance of epic proportions. We rise to our feet and applaud. Desiring an encore, we travel to places where hills and bluffs are arrayed with tiers of overlapping splendor. We are drawn toward a horizon of celestial beauty. The beauty we witness begets a spirit of wonder and reverence. We vest ourselves with gratitude, bow our heads, and prayerfully whisper, "Amen."

During our outings, my mother's memories of and reflections on autumn were infused with contentment, but summer still reminded her of heat and humidity, even though her emotional reaction had softened. When she described closing the windows and pulling down shades as the sun made its way around the sky, I would appreciatively remind her of how her food choices and meal preparation kept us and the house cool. She did talk about the fans and the ways she tried to make life more tolerable by positioning them throughout the house. I could detect some satisfaction as she dwelt on her ingenuity and perseverance. She gratefully spoke about the pleasures of air conditioning and how it allowed her to take back her life during the months of June, July, and August.

I occasionally look back at those summers, imagining the oscillating fan creating a pathway of comfort as its breeze rotated around the room. The effect was similar to that of the wind through a tree on a still summer day, causing the tree branches to wave gently. We are drawn to the beauty of flowers nodding their heads in a breeze, by a stream rippling as a breeze dances across its surface. Our skin is soothed by a gentle breeze. Our hair is ruffled in a breeze, reminding us of times when it was ruffled by tender and appreciative hands. A breeze can slip between and through the spaces left open in God's creation and leave pleasurable traces of itself behind.

A fan was a condition for better living when I was growing up. Its mere presence created expectations of relief, and its actual operation made life comfortable and bearable. We could count our blessings as we were rescued from the seemingly endless days of summer heat and humidity.

Gratitude requires little prompting
when we stand directly in its path.

I like to think of a fan in an anthropomorphic sense too. Like a breeze created by nature, the fan's breeze is generous. It proves to be a blessing in our lives, particularly during the oppressive days of July. There is always enough air to go around. The fan's blades create a pleasing presence that makes everything else better. It transforms uncomfortable conditions, allowing us to carry out our daily tasks.

Likewise, we are often at our best when we do what comes naturally. Yet, we spend much of our lives trying to figure out what others expect of us. We set out to reach our destination but are never quite sure where it is. As with the weather, maybe we need to do the best with what we have. Sometimes people will approve and welcome what we have to offer. At other times, they will complain because it doesn't measure up to expectations. We can be as fickle as the weather itself. Our loyalties are mixed and contribute to the way we greet the day and each other.

Fans once served as useful and reliable weapons in our war against heat and humidity. We were content to use them to drive away the uncomfortable effects of summer weather. But we had to be in the path of the breeze to benefit from its passing by. A balance between staying cool and staying put was not easy to achieve. We had to prevent feeling like hostages in our homes and at the same time minimize the irritability that comes from experiencing disagreeable conditions.

Air conditioners came on the scene like the cavalry in a Western movie. We were no longer held captive in our own homes. When we feel better, we behave better. One piece of manufactured equipment changed our outlook and our disposition during the terrible days of summer.

*Gratitude connects what matters
to what we can do about it.*

Like weather, individuals can create conditions.
Comfort functions like a condition because it is an act of
the will: We can decide to be comfortable with our efforts to
become who we want to be if we no longer feel at the mercy
of things we cannot control. When we are comfortable, we
look forward to living and our hearts are eager for adventure. How we feel inside influences our choices and the face
we show to the world. When we show our best selves, who
can refuse being taken into the dance?

When we are comfortable and grateful for who we are,
we are like a breath of fresh air — good to be around. We
are a welcome greeting and hospitable companion. Our conversation reaches out to others, and we listen with a desire
to reciprocate. We rediscover our best qualities — vital-
ity, sincerity, honesty, and mutuality — ones that invite us
into common endeavors. Faithful adherence to amicability,
civility, and authenticity elevates the effects of our contentment. We become partners in an open spirit of dialogue and
engagement. We are good weather.

We can be hospitable to ourselves if we think of ourselves as being a guest in our own home. We are invited
to be at home in our own skin. We honor our intrinsic
goodness and believe it to be something worthy of us. We
gratefully give ourselves away without the expectation of a
return, believing there will always be enough gratitude to
generously supply others. We only need to make gratitude a
habit of the heart and the mind.

Gratitude is also a condition that rescues us from taking the good things of life for granted. It is so easy to think
we deserve what we get and have. We even think we are
entitled to something more and are disappointed when one

good thing does not follow another. We just expect life to continue delivering. Gratitude prepares us to deal with the setbacks reminiscent of earlier times, when life was more consumed with how to survive each day. We were grateful beyond words when a remarkable turn of events elevated the ordinary to joy. Gratitude for the here and now, an awareness of how good we have it, sharpens our appreciation for life. It brightens the day and leaves an afterglow at night.

Gratitude is most liberating when it is interwoven into one's life and freely given away. There is no need to withhold its power to comfort because its supply is unlimited. When we decide to offer gratitude to others, regardless of their station and condition in life, we have chosen to give and be what people of goodwill cannot misconstrue. Gratitude is a boundless attitude accompanied by a corresponding action that opens doors to the essence of living well.

Gratitude imbues life with happiness. Like an air conditioner, it creates an appetite for living. We feel like we can set a goal and draw upon energy reserves to accomplish it. We do not deplete our energy by using it to make the best of a miserable situation. We can be hospitable to ourselves and pleasant to others. As a thermostat prompts an air conditioner to start, gratitude takes cues from our surroundings to favorably adjust our attitudes and actions.

Gratitude has its limits, just as a fan cannot have the same effect as an air conditioner. Even under the best of conditions, gratitude cannot replace conditions essential to our willingness and desire to be present to others. Gratitude can be our salvation during hard times and the impetus for an intervention to make others' lives more agreeable. It can be a catalyst for mercy and justice when charitable action is sorely lacking. Gratitude can be a standard bearer for those who are voiceless. It points the way, but must be served by those who see and embrace the way.

Gratitude is often an attitude in search of an appropriate outlet for service.

Gratitude serves as a guest of the heart and communion for the soul.

REFLECTION TODAY

A condition creates a space for people to enter and make use of themselves. Kindness, patience, and compassion are examples of conditions. We often think of virtues as conditions; by their nature, they motivate us to do or be something more. A condition can encourage individuals to be and do their best. Ask yourself how you can be a condition that brings out the best in another person. Consider how gratitude may enter and elevate that person's life goals because of the way you inspire an experience of gratitude. Use the condition you have chosen to select appropriate ways to deliver a potentially powerful experience of gratitude for someone else. Act accordingly and reflect upon the results of evoking an experience of gratitude for you as the host and another as a guest.

REFLECTION TOMORROW

Reflect upon the condition you were yesterday. How did your decision and choice of actions promote an experience of gratitude for someone else? What were the fruits of your serving as a condition for an experience of gratitude? How might you make this experience the basis for choosing and doing other conditions that culminate in gratitude?

CHAPTER 11

Waiting

*Gratitude elevates the therapeutic
benefits of waiting.*

We are a nation of hectic seekers caught up in a whirl-
wind of events and a swirl of ideas. Every day we burst into
frenzied activity. We don't leave much space between an
idea and the corresponding actions and often make decisions without reflecting upon the long-term consequences.
We feel useless when we are not doing something productive and have a driving need to be relevant. We make few
provisions for rest. We fail to keep in touch with who we are
and what we are about. We struggle with our self-importance, stuffing ourselves with accomplishments.

We never seem to have enough time, which we equate
with money. Time is the currency we use to purchase
the future. It becomes a tyrant that insists on squeezing
everything out of us in the name of success. We measure
ourselves, and honor others, by how much we own. We live
lives of addition and we can never have too much.

Prior to retirement, I traded time for opportunities to
prove my worth and build a future. There was always so
much work to do, and I poured myself into my job. I listened

to the proponents of excellence, adopting their strategies for success. With the ever-present pressure to get things done, I disliked delays and disruptions. Like many other Americans, I often hurried to get where I was going and even before I got there, I was planning where I would go next. I frequently felt I was not doing enough and consequently was a disquieting figure to those around me.

I am now beginning to understand that standing still at the crossroads of an event or activity can be a useful way to connect with life and consider what doesn't immediately meet the eye. I am trying to reduce the stimuli competing for my attention and create quiet moments among an avalanche of activities, to free myself from nagging reminders to get things done and from work-dominated attitudes. These shifts in perspective have made me more prepared to make mindful decisions, to be more attentive to the natural cadence of life, and to take in the full sweep of a landscape.

I am learning to be more patient, less error-prone, and more content. Waiting is a recess, a suspension of activity, I take to rest and catch my breath. I am learning to trust tomorrow by resting in the middle of my busyness. I have incorporated into my life lots of events that require waiting, and I use these oases of quiet to reflect upon ways not to be productive. I use the time to re-introduce myself to fruitful features of gratitude.

One particular activity that tests my patience is grocery shopping. It illustrates how I have gradually turned waiting into an asset and the basis for ongoing experiences of gratitude. My first encounter with waiting is the meat counter, where I am generally greeted with a friendly, "May I help you?" Gratitude for being next is partially offset by having to wait to secure one item at a time. Waiting here feels like a waste of time, but it is not unduly troublesome. By contrast, moving along collecting items on the list seldom requires waiting. Not until I get to the checkout area does waiting often become a serious issue.

My disposition directs me to approach my choice of line like a private eye looking for clues. There are some obvious "holding-up the line" clues: the number and type of items in a cart, the concentration of the cashier, and the nimbleness of the fellow sacking groceries. These are almost infallible indicators of wait time. A good cashier is able to engage in idle chatter with the customer while performing other essential functions. She deftly sorts items such as chips, bread, and eggs that can be crushed or broken, from crush-resistant items. She clears the way for items to be scanned without losing a beat while agilely grouping items by size and weight. The scanner beeps create a steady rhythm that reflects her efficiency.

This effective delivery system seldom produces results when a small child accompanies an adult in a grocery store. All too often the store management tempts the child with an attractive confectionary display strategically placed at just the right height by the checkout lane. The adult tries to be oblivious to the child rummaging through the candy in front of the cash register. I am not. There is going to be a delay as the parent is drawn into a contest of wills. Children know when they have a distinct advantage and are likely to press their claim after the first "no." They implicitly understand that the adult will feel that his or her parenting skills are subject to evaluation by others in the line and will want to avoid any delay or embarrassment. The adult knows, in light of past experience, that another "no" is likely to be met with utter defiance. I look disapprovingly at the child. The adult sees an ally and, refusing to be intimidated, says, "No!"

Gratitude applauds the proper exercise of authority.

I am generally attracted to a line where I see a person with very few grocery items. Occasionally, I misjudge the situation and become the victim of unforeseen problems. For example, when an item cannot be electronically scanned, someone has to be dispatched to find the price. Or when a customer has been unable to find an item, someone is sent to secure it. Or when a customer returns an item, a receipt is required before a cash reimbursement can be made. Or an authorization must be secured from the manager before a person can write a check. These small delays are inconvenient and provoke aggravation. So many unpredictable conditions can affect my waiting in line.

I have been working at investing this time with thoughts of gratitude. As I return the grocery list to my pocket, I remind myself this list represents economic prosperity, security, and stability. I am grateful I can afford to purchase these items without worrying about their cost. Gratitude adds flavor to the contents of these blessings.

At other times, I pay attention to the items as I remove them from my shopping basket and watch them march along a conveyer belt. On some occasions I concentrate on the ingredients for a particular meal. I think of the people whose labor produced and transported the cereal, the milk, and the fruit that grace my breakfast. I begin each day thankful that some cultivate and harvest the fields of grain, others pasture and milk the cows, and still others bend over in the heat of a day to supply me with the berries that add color and flavor to the meal. My waiting is hardly comparable to that of the producers who must wait for suitable growing and harvesting conditions. I wait, being able to predict the outcome; their wait is subject to conditions they cannot control.

Gratitude functions as a soundtrack keeping us in touch with our blessings.

I have recently begun to offset my distaste for waiting in line in the grocery store by trading on opportunities to visit with people I meet there. Rather than being in a hurry to collect the items on my list, I am reframing the grocery store experience. I began thinking about using grocery shopping to reconnect with people I seldom see elsewhere.

My wife and I have lived in the same community most of our adult lives. We have come to know many people through our various activities. We have been included in the lives of a number of families, and some members have become good friends. We receive birth and baptism announcements and wedding invitations. Our calendars have included pending community events, organization meetings, volunteer assignments, and civic responsibilities. We have built a community while living in one.

We have gone through many stages in the evolution of our friendships and family activities. Retired, we spend less time outside our home. There are fewer chances to meet people whose activities only occasionally intersect with ours. Our friends are also aging, and many have curtailed their activities due to ill health and just plain lack of stamina. We miss the naturally occurring, keeping-in-touch activities of a former day.

People are teaching me to take an intermission attitude when I go grocery shopping. I prepare myself to wait while renewing a friendship or an association. I await some indication that they would like to stop and visit. Verbal and nonverbal clues are like traffic lights — we stop or go depending upon the color of the situation. A green light is a signal to go ahead with the pleasure of exchanging stories.

In this situation I imagine waiting as listening. When we are truly engaged during a conversation, we are attentive to what is being said. Our eyes and posture reveal our pleasure. We wait for the other person to give us some indication they are at a stopping point in their remarks before we offer ours. We often appreciatively pick up on something they have said and target our remarks accordingly. Their remarks serve as reference points for continuing our conversation. Waiting is a centerpiece in the exchange; it is a crucial element in any conversation where both parties feel heard and appreciated. We are grateful when our telling is uninterrupted and we are given the benefit of a full telling of what we have to offer.

Wait time in a conversation is not easy. We are quick to pick up on something that touches who we are and what we have done. We want to introduce these reminders while they are still pertinent. We are also inclined to jump in when the other party has exceeded the limits of our patience or dwells too long on topics we believe to be superfluous. Anxious to keep things moving, we may not wait long enough and prematurely cut the other person off. There is a delicate balance between waiting to hear and waiting to tell. Learning to measure and mediate the distance between these two conventions helps us cultivate friendships.

I have been trying to take my attitude of gratitude into other situations where waiting is a frequent experience. One of these for me is the doctor's office. Although I am given a card noting the date and time for my appointment, I know it only means I am responsible for being present then. It is understood the doctor may not see me at that time. I must be prepared to patiently wait until the doctor has attended to other patients. The inconvenience of waiting is to be offset by the doctor giving me the full benefit of his

time when it is my turn. I have actually been the benefi-
ciary of this understanding.

I believe the medical profession has begun to take
more seriously the relationship between doctor and patient.
The conditions that build and sustain good relationships
include convenience and consideration. Although healing
does not necessarily occur on a schedule, keeping one is an
antidote to impatience and a patient's ill will.

The sign posted in the reception area of my doctor's
office reads, "If you have waited more than fifteen minutes
beyond your appointment time, please notify the reception-
ist." That does make the waiting in the reception area more
predictable, which is good. Although I do not know how
many are ahead of me, I know I will be taken seriously in
no more than fifteen minutes. There is no such sign in the
examination room. However, I feel the doctor has been put
on notice. He will get to me when he can. I am more willing
to wait my turn. Maybe I feel better because I know there
is a system, which, though not perfect, does favor healing.
The wait time may be unpredictable, but knowing time
will finally be on my side makes the wait tolerable if not
acceptable. I have also learned prayer makes for patient
endurance. Prayer time is definitely a healthy way to use
wait time when preparing to see the doctor. Being properly
disposed is essential to receiving and accepting what is
being offered.

Gratitude waits until a path opens to somewhere worth going.

Actually I have tried to use prayer as a way to make
waiting a productive use of time. I suppose my attitude toward waiting is more about the use of time than
the aggravation of standing or staying in one place. It is

rethinking the way I look at time, particularly my earlier outlook on life, which predisposed me to make time a commodity and its use a matter of commerce. But time is not just something we exchange for something of worth; time is not necessarily a unit of work used to produce something that can be bought and sold. Standing in line, waiting for something to happen, doesn't produce anything that can be traded on the open market. We are so accustomed to thinking of time as money that it is hard to imagine waiting as a useful way to make anything worthwhile happen.

Yet, waiting can be put to productive use. Waiting doesn't equate with idleness. Our mind can operate while we are standing in line or sitting down without anything particular to do. It can be a resource available to us for any number of cognitive transactions. We can retrieve things from the past, collect things currently on our mind, or take a visionary look into the future. We can merge the unique benefits of each of these time frames and direct our thoughts toward some desirable purpose.

Waiting can be a place we go to improve and appreciate our relationships with others. We can also use the time to consider what is happening on the fringes of each day. We often relegate people and events to the borders of our lives because we can't get around to doing everything we want to do. While waiting, we can take some notice of these situations. We can turn the pages of our life to remind us of times and people we haven't seen or heard from for a while, others who we know are about to celebrate a special event, and still others we know who are struggling with misfortune or ill health. People in these situations may be waiting to hear from us. While we wait, we can visit someone in the hospital with our prayers. We can mentally reintroduce ourselves to someone who has been particularly special at some point in our lives. If someone has invited us to a celebration, we can take the time to reflect on the person. We can use our waiting to compose a letter or prepare for a telephone call. The message may include a special event or period of time when we were more involved in each other's lives. These are a few of the countless ways waiting can put us in touch with feelings and thoughts that serve as contact points with significant people and events in our lives.

Gratitude can be a midwife putting new life in our relationships.

Words can also serve as a midwife, waiting to help give birth to an idea. This book is the outgrowth of an idea waiting to be born. I began to grow the idea as a parent telling stories to our children and grandchildren. The stories were to be rooted in gratitude because I believe personal stories can serve as a seedbed for growing thoughts about gratitude and its place in a well-grounded life. Gratitude, I feel, is both impetus for and mainstay of all other virtues. These thoughts transformed waiting to write a book into a singleness of purpose and driving force.

I had waited long enough. I previously had written a college textbook and learned the importance of scheduling time periods for writing. I had found ways to sandwich writing in among other activities, for example, while waiting for my wife, a musician in the New Horizons Band, a group of seniors from a variety of backgrounds and musical talent. Her required early arrival before concerts led me to find a quiet place to write prior to taking my seat in the auditorium. Once settled, I organized my thoughts, and searched for the appropriate words, which do not always come when summoned. I would corral some of them as they made their appearance and cajole them into staying around until I could decide upon their usefulness.

I often think I know what I want to say, but I can't find the words to help me say it. I try to coax them out of their hiding places, but the more I try to take control of the situation, the more they resist. I realize word choices do involve some power and control issues. I wait for just the right word combinations to come along; some words are distinctive and "fit the bill" better than others.

Like an editor, I like to give orders to words and make them fall into patterns that suit me, and I am grateful when they oblige. Perhaps you have found while reading these words that some words speak to you with clarity, introducing you to a new way of listening to your ideas and using your voice. At other times my words may come up short in your view. When my words do not produce a thought or a practice that advances your understanding and appreciation of gratitude, or suggest ways to honor it with a commitment, please wait until my words catch up with where you are or where you want to go. Words stand still so you can choose your own thoughts, set your own pace.

I continue to use words to understand, experience, and make friends with gratitude. Words and friendship require a generous investment of time, patience, and understanding. Waiting at a traffic light, at a road construction site, or at a busy intersection provides an opportunity to gather thoughts that make gratitude a friend. We are mindful of people who help us ambitiously greet the day, elevate our purpose, and join in the celebration of our accomplishments. As I dwell on these experiences, gratitude is reignited and savored. Then it can become a catalyst for helping someone meet a project deadline, overcome the limits of their ability, or provide them the motivation to get started on a long-delayed undertaking. Gratitude becomes both a means and an end, an intention and an outcome, helping us to live a more integrated and wholesome life.

Gratitude brings a fresh, functional perspective to waiting. We position ourselves to make waiting a constructive use of time, not an undesirable interruption in our lives. We view it as a windfall and invest it with thoughts and practices rooted in gratitude. We make ourselves available in a wide range of helping situations, some of which arise from happenstance — opening a door, lightening a load, assisting a stranger, or complimenting another's kindness. These short-lived events fuel our desire to use gratitude in other intentional ways. Waiting time can be spent incorporating gratitude into our work and play.

Waiting in lines or offices can actually be a blessing. Time slows down so we embrace it and use it to take care of unfinished business. We stay in place long enough to reflect on the unfinished aspects of caring that seldom get enough of our attention. Gratitude flourishes in situations where time waits on us and does our bidding. Then, we become agents of what matters.

Waiting can be an interior pause to discern the purpose of gratitude, discover its unique contribution, and form intentions to live it more fully. One can reflect on gratitude as a virtue. What is it about gratitude that makes my life more sustainable and secure? How does gratitude influence the way I treat others and extend the benefits of this condition in my life? Why should I be grateful despite hardship and suffering in my life? Who are the people I cherish and thank? There are endless ways we can question the meaning, significance, and extent to which gratitude occupies and plays itself out in our lives. We can remain in readiness and equipped to make gratitude a working partner with all other values that define us.

Gratitude serves as a passport to the well-being of others.

We should be grateful for our ability and capacity to wait. We can learn to suspend time and withhold our involvement in something new. We can refuse to be scheduled for something more to do. The in-between time can be used to grow ourselves into the persons we want to be. Sometimes we have to wait for:

- Permission to step away from duty;
- Grieving to take leave of us;
- Complacency to surrender to hope;
- Forgiveness of an act long ago repented of;
- An opportunity to demonstrate what we are able to do;
- Truth to overcome our blindness or obstinacy;
- Playfulness to remind us all is not work;
- A rainbow to stretch a band of color across the sky;
- Humility to teach us how to forgive; or
- Winter to yield to spring.

Sometimes we wait to:

- Withdraw from a longtime commitment;
- Make use of the fragile moments in our life;
- Surprise someone with an unexpected gift;
- Discover the downside of our exaggerated self-importance;
- Rest a weary body or troubled heart;
- Harvest food from a garden;
- Declare our commitment to a controversial program;
- Taste the fruits of our labor;
- Hold a newborn child;

- Discover who we are in relation to others;
- Understand the meaning and purpose of hardship;
- Deal with the resistance of others;
- Offer an explanation of unbecoming behavior; or
- Recover from surgery.

Sometimes when we wait to and wait for, new life emerges in wonderful life-giving and life-enriching ways. Each day brings forth its own beauty and bounty, and we gratefully appropriate the blessings. Waiting becomes an asset worthy of our commitment. Time may not always be on our side, but we can learn to bide our time and savor its benefits.

Gratitude animates
and exalts goodness.

REFLECTION TODAY

We have places where we sit and wait. Offices, transportation terminals, and hospitals most readily come to mind. In their waiting rooms, we wait until called upon.

We have places where we stand and wait, such as checkout lines in stores. We wait until it is our turn.

Recall one of these places where you have waited recently and what you did while waiting. Note the advantages and disadvantages of not using this time for what you would have otherwise been doing. How might you have made better use of this waiting time? What ways has this chapter noted ways to use gratitude to offset your impatience while waiting and/or to use waiting as a way to grow thoughts of gratitude? What has this chapter offered to increase the likelihood you will use waiting to learn something about gratitude?

REFLECTION TOMORROW

Look back at your responses to yesterday's questions. Do your responses include any thoughts or feelings that suggest waiting can actually be a productive use of time?

Do your responses suggest you are more favorably disposed to think of and use waiting as a desirable condition in your life?

Think about waiting as taking time away from something else you might be doing now. Put the something else aside. Put gratitude on the front burner, and wait for it to warm your heart and inspire something worthy of its presence in your life.

CHAPTER 12

Imagination

Gratitude appreciates expansive and cultivated imaginations.

Fascination is often taking the time to see beneath, behind, and beyond what is right in front of us. Some years ago, we were dealing with a road construction project in our part of the city. Traffic was being rerouted through adjacent residential areas. At the outset, stop signs and detour signs were sufficient cues for directing traffic, but when these were no longer sufficient, a woman was stationed at the intersection to direct traffic. I became engrossed with the way she masterfully diverted traffic.

I began to imagine her standing on a podium, responding to the rise and fall of notes on a musical score, and adjusting her movements to correspond with what she observes and hears. She changes her position and posture as she weighs the contributions of various musicians. There is authority and fluidity in her movements. She doesn't miss a beat. She sees the whole performance and makes provisions for each part as she orchestrates the interaction of the players through the movements of her hands. She is a striking example of believing in what she is doing. She builds on

the unfolding of an event with grace and with uncharacter-
istic fun and flair.

This woman does not appear to be directing traffic.
Rather, she seems to be engaged in the activity around her,
seizing upon the natural flow of events, unpacking the magical moments, and captivating me as an observer. Like an
orchestra conductor, she waves on those who are approach-
ing their place in the performance and holds up those who
are not. She has taken a mundane activity and transformed
the ordinary into a work of art. She observes oncoming traffic, is attentive to arrivals and tries to regulate departures
in a safe and timely fashion. She happens to see the task as
much more than doing something necessary.

Gratitude enhances an event when we let it play its part.

We spend so much of our lives trying to do only what is
absolutely necessary. We invest ourselves in the minimum
and then wonder why there is so little satisfaction in the
results. Most people would regard directing traffic as being
boring. They would be disillusioned if that was all life had
to offer eight hours a day. However, it is not what life offers
us but what we do with what we have been given. Artists
come to mind when I think of making the best of what God
has to offer. It seems to me that artists best exemplify the
acts of creation described in Genesis. As God's first action
was to bring peace and order out of chaos, the artist takes
formless dark and light elements, gives them shape, and
arranges them to produce images.

I do not know what possessed this traffic-control person
to transform herself from a stop- and-go sign to a performing artist, all the while creating order out of potential
chaos. She possessed an imagination that could convert

the humdrum into a work of art. Those under her direction likely wondered about the internal music to which she
swayed and the tempo to which she played.

Gratitude takes the edge off bothersome and troublesome circumstances.

I could not elude one such circumstance when I began
my freshman year at Iowa State Teachers College (now
the University of Northern Iowa). Man and Materials was
included among the required general education classes. Like
many first-generation college students, I had no acquaintance with the purpose of general education nor did I
appreciate being inducted into a program outside my major.
My resistance was anticipated, and this class insisted I find
ways into the idea through hands-on experiences.

This course was designed to introduce students to
the inherent characteristics of the materials artists use to
create a work of art. I was provided the materials and equipment to examine my attitudes and test my skills from the
perspective of an artist. With a block of wood and a chisel,
I was to imagine what I could create and then sculpt an
object. I tried to visualize my block of wood as a cat seated
looking out a window. I had seen a ceramic cat posed this
way. Using a pencil to trace the outline of the figure of a cat
on the face of the block, I tried to chip away the wood that
wasn't part of the cat. The chisel did not cooperate with my
endeavor because the one-dimensional drawing did not supply me with directions to make a three-dimensional object. I
removed enough material from the block of wood to create a
pile of chips, but what remained did not resemble a cat.

The professor, who circulated about the room,
stopped to inquire what I was learning from this exercise.
Other than frustration and humility, I confessed learning

something about the properties of wood, the demands of using a chisel and the difficulties of sculpting a three-dimensional object. He quizzed me about these observations and then told me I could move on to the next project — molding something out of clay.

After the class had completed these two projects, we viewed a slide program on the work of several famous sculptors and potters. A professor who shared his passion and expertise in these two mediums provided the narration. This experience was a wonderful amalgamation of my fledgling experience and that of eminent artists in these two mediums. Similar experiences with printmaking and watercolors expanded the curiosity, appreciation, and understanding I have tried to honor over the years.

I am forever grateful I was required to take Man and Materials, a course that was aptly titled and smartly taught. The students came to understand and appreciate our human capacity to use specialized tools to translate mental images into something never seen before. We learned how materials with malleable properties could be formed and molded into objects of infinite and exquisite design. I became more aware of the ways we are surrounded and formed by beauty. I was able to visualize the process, seize some of the energy, and participate in the creative powers of an artist.

I learned to think of our campus as an art gallery, unpretentiously exhibiting good art. If we paid attention, we could assemble our own collection of favorite pieces. Taking a mental walk across our campus, I can still view the sculptures and images in various buildings, savoring a vast array of esteemed choices.

The class provided me a keen curiosity about art and an ongoing fascination with the mental processes of artists. I have become an emissary for what I learned in this class, particularly as a patron of a local arts festival and, years later, as its co-director. Festival organizers continue to take great pride in creating a welcoming climate for artists as weekend guests. We have established a tradition for creating conversations between the artists and festival patrons and participants. We have greatly profited from this situation. We have been taught to understand what appeals to us and to listen because we are being welcomed inside the lives and work of fascinating people. We often part company without a purchase but with the satisfaction of learning from and enjoying one another.

As I retrace thoughts about my initial, serious exposure to art and note the inroads it has made into my life, I am reminded of a few artists whose novel ways of creating art have appealed to me. Some artists do seem disposed to see beyond the purpose of ordinary objects. My wife and I have been purchasing art at our local arts festival for twenty-nine years. One piece is from an artist with a sensitivity to the 1960s. Her artwork consists of arrangements of grapevines and stones of various size, shape, and color. The grapevines serve as a frame for a nest of stones. Often a single stone is safely tucked into an artistic arrangement of tangled vine. Part of the appeal to me is to see discarded and overlooked objects of nature assembled to produce a whimsical and free-spirited composition. Her language may not speak to everyone, but I am grateful she exposes a part of life that would otherwise be hidden to me. I am intrigued by her willingness to persevere in her presentation of an art form many would dismiss. Although her art does not appeal to everyone, we can be grateful that she believes in what she does and persists.

Gratitude pauses to appreciate the strength and courage to be different.

Another artist of our acquaintance has capitalized on our disposable-oriented society. He has created yard sculptures by welding a variety of small metal objects together. Discarded tools were the centerpiece for a variety of sculptures. The artist fashioned delightful figures from shovels and rakes, affixing pieces to the metal and attaching objects to the wooden handles with wire. He incorporates hammers, wrenches, pliers, picks, nuts and bolts, spark plugs, barbed-wire fencing, metal door handles — whatever one might have to pay to dump and which a dump-site operator would be happy to hand over without cost. It was fun to view his creations and equally enjoyable to stand aside and listen to the reactions of others. He must have been delighted to be the source of so much mirth, joy, and laughter. There was something there for everyone; few passed by without noticing and commenting. I liked being among those who noticed and expressed their connection.

One of our favorite artists, a fellow collegian back in the day, is now an internationally renowned potter and ceramic design artist. At our small college, where everyone knew everyone else by sight if not by name, it was not surprising an attractive go-getting journalist on the college newspaper caught his eye or he hers, resulting in a marriage of more than fifty years and six children. Our collegiate acquaintanceship grew to friendship during their involvement in the College Hill Arts Festival. They set up his pottery exhibit at a triangle intersection of two sidewalks, where browsers would have room to stand back and view his stunning pots. The shape, design, and glaze of each pot featured stories told through ancient and archeological symbolism. He delighted in making each pot

a repository of life in another time and place. Her lyric stories are at once whimsical, beguiling, and philosophical.
They are invitations to enter her reverie and create a story
alongside the one she is telling. They recount her life as an
Iowa farm girl and the landscape beauty of their lives in the
hills and valleys of northeastern Iowa. She also draws us
into her passion for teaching students enrolled in American
Indian and African-American literature courses she
teaches at a community college. There is a fascinating con-
fluence between the topics in her courses and the themes
he addresses in the design of his pottery. They are like a
chemical compound, needing only a question to serve as
catalyst for weaving engaging, entertaining, and enlighten-
ing stories. Together they are bastions of imagination and
charming troubadours for their respective arts.

I must not leave unmentioned the work of another
artist, a high school art teacher married to my youngest
brother. There are plentiful reasons for being grateful she
is a member of the family. Uppermost in this context are
her yearly Christmas, birthday, and anniversary cards.
She has something in common with the two artists I have
already mentioned: She also works with materials with little intrinsic artistic value. Her "card workshop" consists of
simple stock and sheets of colored paper, engraved designs
on textured paper, and paper processed and printed according to her liking. She produces a surprising and fascinating
number of designs for special occasions by cutting and
shaping, assembling and affixing. We have saved these
cards over the years and will one day ask her to help us
assemble a collage we can frame and hang with our growing art gallery.

I have studied the components of her works without
discovering how she so artfully combined them. I suspect
she somehow sees what is unique in each element and

balances and blends the best of what each has to offer. Her artistry seems to begin as a search for treasures — the accumulated wealth tucked away in drawers, stacked on shelves and chairs, stuffed into baskets, and piled on the floor. She selects, merges, and transforms these articles into a work of art by seeing the power of each to contribute to her vision. Like a magician, the artist must decide what to show and what not to show. The result tantalizes the imagination, entertains our sense of wonder, and leaves us wanting more.

Artists illuminate the spaces all around us, inviting us to stay put and absorb the moment. They are restful reminders that life is about both assimilation and accommodation. The transaction between the two increases our appetite to live more fully. We welcome creation vibrating and unfolding. Our imagination has a place to play around. We are pleased with ourselves.

Gratitude can charm and delight us.

We do not own any piece of art that has cost more than five hundred dollars. We do not have more than one piece from a single artist. Every piece has been purchased following a conversation with the artist. We know something about what inspires the work, what was involved in doing the piece we have chosen, and what it is about the work that gives the artist the most satisfaction. Likewise, we share what inspired our decision, what we value about the piece, and what will likely contribute to our enjoyment as we view this piece in our home. This exchange creates a lasting connection with the person who has given us such pleasure. When an artist returns to the festival in subsequent years, we renew our acquaintance. Gratitude becomes an integral part of these relationships.

We have been fortunate to interact with those who have invested part of themselves in creating an artistic piece. These conversations have been the impetus for multiple experiences of gratitude. We are at once grateful we stopped by an artist's booth, that we were immediately attracted to the work; that we took the time to look, listen, and learn that we could afford to make the purchase; and that our decision has been validated over and over again. It is not just being grateful for what now belongs to us. It is also gratitude for being part of the way a few talented people make a living, for their generous and patient willingness to help us discover what they bring to their work and take from sharing it with others. The price we pay for a work of art cannot adequately appreciate or compensate the artist.

Gratitude can help bridge the gap between the intrinsic and extrinsic motives and values that bind us together. Gratitude does not operate on the economic principle of supply and demand. Rather, gratitude can be given away without fear of not having enough. The real problem lies in our taking too much for granted or neglecting to see that the price we pay is only the beginning of the transaction. The aftermath of gratitude is feeling good about what we have and who we are.

In some way we are all traffic-control persons — we have to keep in touch with everything going on all around us. We come to lots of intersections and have to decide whether to go straight, turn left, or turn right. We can easily become distracted or disoriented and head off in the wrong direction.

Maybe we can pay attention to where we are going and still appreciate the sights and sounds all around us. Maybe we need to listen to the music beneath the activity and use the score to point ourselves in the right direction. The woman directing traffic believed in what she was doing and put her whole self into doing it. She used the music in her mind and heart to help us imagine the music that was there. We could see the evidence, and it lightened our day and made us partners in the dance. There are many ways she could have gotten the job done, but she chose a way that gave us the pleasure to pause and to see the way that made a difference. We could not help but be amused and entertained.

Life is what we make of it, and gratitude makes more of life. The traffic-control woman and the artist serve as mentors for our imagination's seeing. They can best perform their craft when we take time to look. They have to stop time in its path to allow us to imagine and appreciate. We have to put time in our budget if we are to appreciate what is going on all around us. Artists know how to stop us in traffic, to direct us down pathways of imagination, pleasure, and surprise. Unfortunately, when we are so intent upon getting somewhere, we keep our eyes fixed on our destination to the exclusion of all else. The art of living is learning how to balance where we are going with what occurs while getting there.

Gratitude reminds us of priceless favors we almost missed.

REFLECTION TODAY

Imagination is a matter of envisioning what might be or could be. It is letting go of the common and ordinary way of seeing things and making sense of life. Imagination does not worry about what others might think. It tries new and fun-filled ways of getting something done. The intellectual mind plays second fiddle to the affective mind; feelings dominate thoughts.

Embrace imagination and feel the energy of acceptance and trust. Now focus on the creative side of yourself. Imagine the power of fun and adventure that could be yours if you were more inclined to let yourself be more lighthearted. Imagine your way into doing something out of the ordinary, something that will put a little spring in your step. It can simply be changing the order in which you do something, the way you present yourself to others or to yourself, or making something with a fresh and frivolous look. Then do it. Be grateful for having done it regardless of the outcome.

REFLECTION TOMORROW

Yesterday you dove into your imagination and came out of your conventional way of thinking and doing things. You got off the treadmill, took a deep breath and came up with a fresh idea, and did something to put a little zing into your life. What thinking restraint did you have to throw off? How difficult was it to step outside the habit of thinking, "life has always been this way and it is okay"? What did you learn about the relationship between freedom and imagination? About the relationship between gratitude and imagination? What did you learn to appreciate about yourself that will likely contribute to a more accomplished imagination?

CHAPTER 13

Forgiveness

*Gratitude renews a wounded spirit
and transports us beyond our troubles.*

A marriage between gratitude and forgiveness can produce enduring bonds of affection and life-long appreciation. Both conditions must be present if a relationship is to mature and stand the test of time. At times, gratitude comes before forgiveness; a relationship rooted in gratitude may dispose a person to be forgiving. At other times, forgiveness is the handmaiden of gratitude and forms the basis for a recommitment to one another. Gratitude and forgiveness become the solid basis for building and sustaining a relationship.

I met Vic when he was 82 years old and I was 18. He painted farm buildings and needed an assistant. I was looking for a job — almost any job. Fortunately, he asked me just one question about my qualifications: "Do you have any painting experience?" I had helped an uncle paint his small, single-story house some years earlier, so I said, "Yes, I have painting experience." Perhaps desperate for help, Vic didn't question what I told him. I gratefully accepted a job that paid $1 an hour, a wage that today looks like employer abuse. However, with my college fee-exemption scholarship, I paid $33 tuition each quarter. I figured that without any other source of income, in four eight-hour days I could pay for one of the three quarters during my sophomore year of college. I began my first day of work with Vic the following Monday.

Vic quickly learned what little painting experience I had, and I quickly figured out how hard I would work to earn $1 an hour. He did not mention the need to move a 40-foot extension ladder, much less how to position it to maximize my reach on both sides. I didn't mention my second thoughts about misrepresenting myself and taking on more than I could handle. Our relationship began as a truce: We were in this together and would make the best of it.

Gratitude accepts limits by overlooking them.

Moving a paint-laden 40-foot extension ladder required the strength and skill of a weight lifter. Vic's muscular upper body showed the results of decades of this work. I was astonished to see him tilt a 40-foot ladder extended to half its length, lean it back across his huge right shoulder, and transport it from one end of the barn to the other. This feat combined balance, agility, and strength. I gratefully accepted his wise advice and gentle persuasion to execute this maneuver with a 24-foot ladder.

But Vic's lesson did not include how high I would climb to perform my painting duties. My first climb up the 40-foot ladder taught me why Vic hired a younger person for the highest work. I painted the peak of the barn while he painted on the 24-foot ladder halfway down the siding below me. Although he escaped the height, early on he paid quite a price for painting below me. "How could it be raining," he mused, "when the sun is shining without a cloud in the sky?" Vic soon learned to avoid such a downpour if he painted on my right side, where I had much better brush control. In my previous painting experience on an easy-to-move stepladder, I relied exclusively on my right hand — another indication of my inexperience.

Eventually I learned to paint using both hands and to work in between the ladder rungs to efficiently cover a large area without moving the 40-foot ladder. As I learned the job, Vic teased me about getting more paint on myself than on the building. In this way he accepted my inexperience, reassuring me that it was okay. He knew I had much to learn, and he graciously agreed to be my tutor and mentor.

Gratitude makes more of a little something.

Although Vic teased me, he also protected me. When a passing farmer wondered aloud, "Does he get more on himself or the building?" Vic camouflaged his distaste for such a remark with a wide grin and a quick retort, "Come out and watch him for an hour. You will have an answer to that question." He seldom said anything about the amount of paint I laid on the building or myself. He didn't have to. I knew if I could match his output, he would be impressed. And I was out to impress him and covered lots of territory in a day.

True, Vic made painting look easy — 50 years of experience has its advantages. Mine were youthful vigor and a competitive spirit. I desired to please him and prove he had made a good decision to hire me. Our kinship made hot, humid days more tolerable and the growing accomplishment more rewarding. I matured sufficiently to understand what had begun as an employer-employee relationship had evolved into an intergenerational appreciation of one another. Yet at the time I lacked the maturity to recognize the less apparent influences and lessons shaping our relationship while we painted. Only later did I see that the job was as much about making a man as about learning a trade. Vic treated me like a grandson.

Recognition of this status became more evident when I was invited to take the noon meal with Vic and his wife, Carrie. We always took an hour for lunch, and the physical distance from the house we were painting in town to their house was less than a mile. However, the social-psychological distance we traveled has lasted a lifetime. I can still bring back the feelings of being at the center of their affection and appreciation. I can picture the opulence of Carrie's favorite and prized culinary offerings. The aroma that permeated the house was tantalizing. Vic, proud of his wife's cooking, praised her specialty — baked chicken with mashed potatoes and gravy. Tempting to the eye and delightful to the palate, they were an introduction to an assortment of other family favorites. However, nothing drew more praise than her exquisite lemon meringue pie, with its bright yellow filling over a melt-in-your mouth crust topped with deep waves of shiny meringue with lightly browned peaks. I couldn't praise it enough.

Everything about the meal pointed to it being a feast for the mind, body, and spirit. This was no ordinary expression of their desire to cherish and please me. All of this attention, and the intent of this hour, became apparent as Vic and Carrie, seated at each end of the table, looked at me and smiled at one another. They seemed to be savoring this time together and delighting in wonderful me. This was their way of telling me what they had been saying to one another about me and sharing the appreciation that emerged from their conversation. The joy they experienced, and that I reciprocated, has withstood the passage of time and can be revisited by simply uttering their names.

Gratitude nurtures the intangibles that feed us.

Each day Vic and I formed the entire crew. At work we intensely devoted ourselves to the task and seldom engaged in an actual conversation. Rather, our exchanges centered on what we were doing and would do next. During this time, I often thought about our earlier conversations or what we might talk about at lunch. Vic's life was a story unto itself, and he loved to tell it. Long days and many years gave him lots of time for introspection and reflection. I embraced such conversations because I had many similar ones with my dad. Frequently I asked Vic to expand upon a story or explain how happiness and hardship had shaped his life. Curiosity and imagination fueled my questions and constant probing to understand life's ups and downs. Vic's life was quite unlike my current or future one, but it offered invaluable lessons.

Gratitude participates in our life-defining stories.

Fortunately for this line of work, heights didn't bother me much. Still, I remained cautious and attuned to the danger of stretching my body and extending my arms to maximize each setting of that 40-foot ladder. I was a tinge frightened when I moved the ladder without returning to the ground. I did this by bouncing the ladder so it slid slightly to the right onto partially dried painted areas that left a slick veneer. A few times the ladder slid across the painted area and only came to rest when it hit the roof overhang. I held on for dear life as the ladder careened across the surface of the barn, banged up against the overhang, twisted, and shimmied. Generally I could use the roof to steady the ladder and gradually slide it back into place.

Vic gave me good advice early on to "stay with the ladder," particularly if it started falling to the ground. Twice over the course of three summers, I rode the ladder toward the ground and stepped aside immediately before it hit the ground. After those two frightening episodes, Vic sat with me under the shade of a tree for at least 30 minutes. His consideration sufficiently calmed my nerves and helped me create the appearance of "nothing to it." When I climbed the ladder once again, the unpainted area loomed large after the ladder had been reset. The remedy — to resume painting — required more courage than paint.

Gratitude claims our thoughts when we avert a tragedy.

As I look back, I realize much between Vic and me hinged on forgiveness. With justification, Vic might have been upset with my limited painting experience and how much I had to learn. He could have decided I just wasn't going to work out. He could have suggested a reduction in my salary until I served an apprenticeship. Yet he never said or did anything that suggested he felt this way or contemplated any of these solutions. Rather, he seemed to appreciate that I did my best and aspired to get better. Surely he looked at all the positive indications that his decision would work out and placed his bet that it would.

Vic's gamble paid off. My good intentions and work ethic offset my limitations. My motives and his goodwill sealed the bargain without a need to discuss my inexperience. Our reconciliation blended honesty, courtesy, and patience into a workable union. We forged an understanding that valued and appreciated one another.

We are indeed fortunate when forgiveness and thoughtfulness are the cornerstones in a relationship. In building relationships, we trust another's inherent goodness and then discover how to exercise our own. In forgiving others, our own goodness may surface to create something special between us. We feel more at home with one another. With shared goals we gladly cross the threshold to mutual understanding.

We acknowledge the salutary effects of forgiveness and gratitude. Each extends the hand of friendship and reminds us that when these two conditions become companions, peace will follow. Forgiveness supplies the basis for going forward, gratitude the energy to be faithful to the quest.

Gratitude favors those who come in peace.

My vivid recollection of the coalescence of forgiveness and gratitude happened the third summer I worked with Vic. One day as I entered the back door of Vic and Carrie's house, I glimpsed Vic's brand new maroon Chevy pickup in the garage. The garage door was open so I knew Vic had already loaded up painting equipment or made other preparations for the day. Generally he appeared ready to go when I arrived, but not that day. I later realized Vic was intentionally late so he could give me the keys and ask me to back the spankin' new truck out of the garage. At the outset I saw his gesture laden with good intentions and affection.

The rear of the garage opened into an alley with a telephone pole directly across from the garage exit. As I began backing up the truck, I devoted my attention almost exclusively to the potential disaster — backing into the pole

— when actually the garage doorframe was the looming disaster. I cut the wheel too sharply and the front fender grazed the side of the doorframe. Seeing no point in driving back into the garage, I continued into the alley. After turning the motor off, I got out to survey the damage. A sizable dent appeared in the fender, and a few streaks of white paint showed on either side of the dent. I spent the longest two minutes of my life waiting for Vic. I tried to think of ways to undo the damage, but I knew it was too late. Although I don't remember what I said to Vic, I distinctly remember exactly what he said to me. "Len, it is a truck. It will be new for one day," he smiled. "Well, not quite one day." This was the extent of his reaction.

Vic treated this as a minor issue, not a huge tragedy. I wanted him to offer more specific and consoling remarks about the dent or the scrapes, but he let his actions do the talking. However, I kept offering solutions, trying to undo the mistake. I suggested using a rubber mallet to pop out the dent from the underside of the fender — anything to make the dent less obvious. On the contrary, Vic never repaired the damage nor spoke of it again. Some might say he left the dent as a reminder of my negligence or poor judgment, but I knew better. He left the damage untouched to convince me what I had done was no big deal. He said this was just a truck and acted as though it was not meant to be anything more to me.

Gratitude accepts forgiveness as a gift of the heart.

The proximity of gratitude and forgiveness in this poignant encounter with Vic's truck drove home their connection for me. Usually we resist forgiveness because we want time to talk about how terrible we feel. We continue to make amends, even though we may not be able to right the wrong. For instance, I suggested solutions to mitigate or undo some of the damage. But I did not offer additional apologies because Vic closed the door after the first one. His treatment made it absolutely clear that he wanted me to extract "forgiveness" from this situation.

As I tested his sincerity, I saw no contradictions between what Vic said and what he did. This congruence was a measure of his integrity and my dignity. This was indeed about our relationship — not really about the truck. "Things" do not make or sustain relationships. Rather the way we regard others and work with relationships makes a difference. I felt more completely valued during the three summers I worked with Vic. I think he might have felt the same way. Gratitude does remind us of what really matters and of the people who taught us why.

Gratitude grows from the aftermath of unconditional forgiveness.

REFLECTION TODAY

We have all damaged property and relationships. Some of the damage can easily be undone; some cannot. But the residual effect of such damage is difficult to repair and may become the material for forgiveness. One person gathers feelings that form regrets and tries to express them. The other person gathers the feelings of loss and searches for ways to deal with it. Yet these feelings, words, and actions are seldom perfectly aligned. What is left undone or unsaid in the relationship is the material for forgiveness.

Recall an instance in your life when you broke or damaged something that could not be fixed or was never really the same. Remember what you and the other person said and did to make things right between the two of you.

Consider that you both suffered, but neither of you fully understood or fully empathized with the other's grief. Yet, both of you wanted to undo as much of the damage as possible. Recall how you each drew upon forgiveness to reduce the pain and restore health in your relationship. How did gratitude help supply a solution and mend the relationship?

REFLECTION TOMORROW

Forgiveness is not forgetting. In yesterday's situation, you may still harbor some pangs of guilt or feel the other person still mourns the loss. Yet there is nothing more you can say or do, and the other person expects nothing more. How can gratitude help you deal with the imperfect results of forgiveness?

Afterword

Story provides words to look at, listen to, and tell our lives. Gratitude provides a way to tell our story with grace, humility, and joy.

With the advent of TV came the test pattern. Stations used television cameras to adjust, calibrate, and align the signal prior to transmitting it. Viewers used the test pattern to see if they were receiving the signal. While music played in the background, the pattern appeared on the screen until the station began broadcasting content. In the early days, the day's broadcast schedule might precede the first program. Generally, the signoff included playing the national anthem.

Most viewers tried to improve signal reception using a rabbit ear antenna comprised of two slender poles attached to a metal base. The poles could be spread sideways and lifted up and down and the base could be rotated to improve signal reception. Program transmission depended on atmospheric conditions for airwave quality. We learned to depend upon and appreciate the test pattern and rabbit ears during the early years of television broadcasting.

Like a test pattern, the cover of this book was used to transmit a signal. The test pattern included words and images to make you wonder what comes next. I am glad you slowed the pace and tempo of your life to pick up the book and look inside. You probably either paged through the book to examine its contents, or you read a publisher's description online. You were interested enough in the subject matter to purchase a copy. As you read, you listened to my stories and compared them with your own. At times, you may have felt you belonged inside my stories and identified with one or more of the characters. Befriended, we traveled together. We were growing our stories. We were growing our lives.

My stories may have helped you improve the reception of yours. You may have used "rabbit ears" to improve the clarity and quality of what you remembered. Stories became a deliberate way to make gratitude a direction-determining, choice-making, and truth-bearing instrument in your life. Our traveling the length, width, and depth of gratitude has expanded its meaning, stirred a desire to live it more fully and to encounter it at the forefront and afterwards of our lives.

I am grateful you were attracted by the test pattern and decided to include the book in your life. I was thinking about you as I wondered what I could say with my life that would be meaningful in yours. When I decided on gratitude as the topic and theme, I thought you would listen and learn. Thus, at this intersection of our lives, I made a promise to help you make gratitude a centerpiece and mainstay in your life. I hope I have been faithful to the promise and you are pleased and satisfied with what I offered you. Every author hopes that readers feel their life has been made better, more fruitful, fulfilling, and satisfying because the book spoke to them about something they needed or wanted to hear and learn. Like other authors, I began with an audience in mind: people who would tune in and keep the channel open to the message.

Each day, as I wrote this book, I relied upon gratitude for energy. I used it to create a greater awareness of the ways people are the impetus for thoughts and experiences of gratitude. You, as readers, become characters in my story through the counterparts in my life right now — not exact replicas to be sure, but possessing some of the qualities I believe you bring to our story. I found you in friends, acquaintances, and strangers who crisscross my life each day. Today I saw you in the student who pleasantly greeted me when "swiping" my ID card at the wellness center, in two former colleagues whose conversation rescued me from drab and boring repetitive physical activities, a driver who waited for me to back out of my parking space, the cook and waitress who made it possible for me to have an attractive alternative to milk and cereal, and a courtesy telephone call soon after my arrival home reminding me of a dental appointment. And it is only 8 a.m. These people surrounded me with pleasant experiences and told me life is good.

However, even with these simulated introductions to you and so much to be grateful for, there were days when I couldn't get in touch with what you were telling me, days when words stubbornly refused to help me. I was also out of touch with what I was trying to say, like those times when we don't quite know what to say to one another and are at a loss for words to say it. At one of these junctures, I made a startling discovery as I reread the manuscript trying to gather some momentum; I discovered the absence of a topic integral to the full experience of gratitude in our lives — humor. I introduce this brief aside by way of an apology. Of course, I have chosen a story to deal with this unfortunate oversight.

Some people in our lives, by their sheer presence, evoke a sense of fun and playfulness. These people often become the centerpiece of a prank or a good joke. Our mischievousness is fueled through anticipating their laughter.

One such person in my life was a colleague. We enjoyed surprising him by inventing an offbeat event or by an exaggerated use of a holiday. Christmas was a perfect time to put in place some outrageous ways to catch him off guard. One year we secured the keys to his office and decorated it with outlandish articles collected from a St. Vincent de Paul thrift store. All the articles celebrated a Christmas theme; some were used to decorate an artificial tree, others were beautifully gift-wrapped and tastefully placed on a decorative skirt at the base of the tree. We gazed upon the scene as shoppers viewing the Christmas window display at Macy's department store. To say we were proud would be an understatement.

This was final exam week. Knowing the guest of honor would come in about an hour ahead of time, we assembled in an office across the hall from his. We heard him unlock his office door, then roar with laughter, saying, "Okay, you guys, where are you?" He knew we could not be far off. We could not resist the opportunity to witness the moment of his discovery and take part in the banter and horseplay that would follow.

Since it was Christmas, he had to open the gifts, which were supposedly from various university dignitaries whose very names suggested his impressive credentials. The comments on the cards spoke of some aspect of their esteem for him, and we had a hilarious time noting the dubious truth of their observations. The unwrapped gifts were assembled and displayed under the tree to showcase our ingenuity and invite others to join the fun. Throughout the day the hallway was the scene of a series of festive gatherings. We greeted the season with a chorus of laughter and goodwill.

There are many ways, creatively and playfully, to connect the dots between humor and gratitude. Often the impetus begins by finding someone we seriously like and telling them so in a nonserious way. I am grateful for having these people in my life. I imagine some of you are similarly grateful and blessed to make such people the brunt of a good-natured joke that provokes infectious laughter and joy.

Gratitude may be a leaning toward the serious, sometimes causing us to become too intent on making it an ongoing expression of our lives and subverting joy in the process. It is wise to remember that the learning curve involved in everything begins simply and involves living ourselves into a habit, then believing our lives into a commitment. Humor helps us achieve some balance in our outlook on life and keeps us from taking life and ourselves too seriously. It is a good antidote for the "should haves" and "ought tos" that contribute to ingratitude. Gratitude does not insist on being our companion and tutor, but it loves the invitation and thrives on the welcome.

Throughout this book I have used story to elevate and reinforce your intention to make gratitude a lifestyle choice; I have discussed the gratitude growth potential and offshoot effects of each story. In the process, I have felt we were becoming connected at the hip. I imagined we were making gratitude a linchpin in our relationship and an essential element in our identity. I imagined gratitude summoning us to greater appreciation of each other and encouraging us to count our blessings. Gratitude became a gift-bearing voice challenging us to live more fully in the present while helping us recover from setbacks, stretching us beyond your insecurities, and leaving us confident about the future. Gratitude became a peacemaker and left an imprint of well-being and solidarity. Each story became an honest exchange of goodwill. I also came to visualize gratitude as a seamless garment we would wear as an article of faith in one another. We would be forever changed by subscribing to the ideal and using it to make our lives better and tell our stories.

All authors stand inside a blessing when a reader takes their labor seriously and puts some part of themselves inside their work. I trust you will continue to make gratitude a focal point in your life and let it become your mentor as you grow yourself into its extravagant possibilities. I hope you will use the reflections as incubators of ideas and thoughts, as inquisitive counterpoints to my thoughts, leading to new insights and conclusions. I hope you will regard this book as a purposeful and principled look at life through the lens of gratitude; and that gratitude, when used in conjunction with other virtues, will become a life worthy of you. And to this end, I close with a blessing:

May gratitude be a first cause and

instance of caring for all of creation.

May gratitude be a Holy Grail

of blessings in your life.

May gratitude be a presence that

inspires hope and elevates joy.

Amen

Reading Group and Self-Directed Study Extras

Q&A with Author Len Froyen

Q *Identify a particular life event or experience that caused you to begin to think deeply about gratitude.*

A When my wife broke her upper humerus falling on ice in the winter of 1999, her recuperation after surgery required some radical changes our lives. Her health care required changes in my daily schedule and my availability to her. There were so many previously simple tasks she could no longer do without help that required new sensitivities and forms of consideration on my part. Initially I made a habit of thinking of the demands as "pay back" time, an opportunity to reciprocate for the incredible ways she had encouraged and supported me when I was preparing to become a deacon and when fulfilling the educational requirements of a doctoral program. Gradually the health care routine yielded to other ways of relating to each other. We began to be more aware and to think more deeply about the ways love and gratitude had previously preserved and enriched our marriage; also how all too often we were unmindful and unappreciative. Being more attentive to the unique ways we needed and celebrated each other produced a groundswell of appreciation. Gratitude served as a relationship-building attitude and care-taking commitment.

Q *How has reading the work of other authors influenced your understanding and approach to gratitude?*

A I read several books that became "starting points" in appreciating the power of gratitude as a guide to make and remake my life. I was most impressed and influenced by Mary Jo Leddy's *Radical Gratitude.* She asked the provocative question, "If you could say your life with one word, what word would you choose?" After providing a list of potentially evocative words, she said she would choose gratitude. I became fascinated with the task — and relationship-orientated ramifications of this choice.

Q *Family stories seem deeply important to your experience of gratitude. Provide another example to underscore this point.*

A The grandmother whose story was not included in the book was the mother of fifteen children. She was pregnant off and on for about twenty-two years. I listened to her story during vacation visits. Her life focused on the daily, and was simple and demanding. Yet I saw her as serene and joyful. Prayer and a deep, active devotion to the Virgin Mary connected these two aspects of her life. Serenity was thankfully and calmly living in the present; joy was sharing her cinnamon bread, much to the delight of all.

Q *How does our family story provide models of gratitude?*

A Our families help us make good stories. At their best, they model gratitude as a way of sharing their stories. The stories re-introduce us to one another, take us inside our lives, and disclose what holds us together. The "remember the time we" puts the story in a relational context; the topic and details evoke our feelings, which become a subtext for our stories. I think feelings are the best source for retrieving what matters to us. We were feeling animals long before mind/cognition gave our feelings a place to reside. We go "back home" to collect our stories and use our feelings to reconstruct what our home (our dwelling place) is like. Gratitude is a good place to be when spending time with our family.

Q *Describe a time when your own failure to react*
with gratitude caused you regrets or grief.

A My paternal grandmother would faithfully send me a birthday
card and one dollar during my late childhood and adolescent
years. My parents did not remind me or insist I send her a
thank-you note. The card was just a card and a dollar didn't
mean much to me. My evaluation of the gift crushed the
sentiment with which it was sent. I can now imagine how
much a brief, even if not sincere, thank you would have
meant to her. There are some things in life we can't do over.
Gratitude is best when it keeps up with the good that is going
on every day.

Q *How do you believe gratitude heals wounds in families?*

A Gratitude heals wounds in families by using stories with
thankful themes. When my twenty-one year old brother was
killed in an automobile accident, our family took solace in
the good things that had most recently defined his life and
were sources of happiness. The conversation created a circle
of strength and understanding. We gathered the emotional
resources to touch the pain of loss. Pain was shared in the
context of our having gone through the ups and downs of
life together. We became sacraments of healing by anointing
each other with comforting words and embraces of love.

Q *Can the practice of telling stories be strong enough*
to instill an important character trait like gratitude?

A We do not learn character traits in the abstract. Our behavior
forms who we are. Stories provide us with inspiration and
concrete examples. We learn to do life and come to be who
we are. We can choose our place in various stories and use
them to tell ours. It is in the telling that we put flesh on our
affirmation of self and better tell ourselves to others. The
birth and life of a good story is often rooted in prized virtues.
We want to be prized for our virtues and honor those of others.
Gratitude is a virtue with an appealing storyline as it has a
"Happy Birthday" feel to it.

Q *Isn't teaching gratitude the work of religion?*

A The content of gratitude belongs to everyone and everyone should be a gift-bearer of it. None of us are exempt from expressing, sharing, and living by it. Whereas gratitude should be a foremost teaching of religion, it is but one of the church's evangelization activities. Were the inculcation of gratitude the sole responsibility of religion, its reach would be limited; its instruction would be unavailable to many.

Q *How does gratitude stack up against other virtues?*

A Gratitude is the seedbed for other virtues. Plant the seeds of other virtues in the soil of gratitude and they will yield a bountiful harvest. Other virtues are rooted in and nourished by gratitude. Gratitude is like perfume; it leaves traces of itself wherever it goes.

Q *How well does gratitude fit into in a culture of excess, where we are seldom content with what we already have?*

A Our constant striving for more of everything contributes to discontent, stress, anxiety, and occasional bouts with depression. Advertising and marketing press us into believing possessions are a pathway to happiness. We can buy the message and purchase their solutions to a good life, but our acquisitive motives and consumption activities often become our downfall. Gratitude is a life-style decision that serves as a moral hedge against greed and its companions, pride and power.

Q *Is there a downside to gratitude and those who are proponents of it?*

A Gratitude can be a scapegoat for those who claim it stifles initiative. Gratitude is countercultural in an economy dependent on freewheeling spending and the use of credit cards to purchase the future. Because gratitude generally disposes and equips us to generously give away our savings to support the basic needs of others, proponents of gratitude can sometimes be viewed as self-righteous and lacking in humility. They may also be seen as bolstering their feelings of superiority by standing in judgment of the perceived selfishness or lack of initiative of others.

Q *Why did you write a book about gratitude?*

A I want people to have a broad and deep experience of gratitude in their lives. Gratitude can be experienced at many different levels. At the most superficial level, it is politeness, the thank-you habit we are taught as children. At another level, it can be pleasant and genuine; one's voice conveys its sincerity. At a deeper lever, there is gratitude in a present moment when all of life seems to be going as planned, yielding contentment and peace. There is gratitude that reaches back in time and makes a connection with something meaningfully and appreciatively experienced all over again. Gratitude may be coming to know ourselves in a new way or someone else in a more personal and profound way. It may be the faithfulness of others when life tests our strength to cope, our capacity to hope. It may be like a mystical experience where we feel at one with all creation. Or it may be having the ability to give away something dear to us because we believe it may matter more to someone else. We go deeper into gratitude when we learn and act upon our capacity to surrender, to trust. I hope somewhere in my stories, the reader will enter these deeper levels of gratitude and find within my stories trigger points to deepen experiences of gratitude in their stories. I want people to have a pervasive experience of gratitude in their life choices. Gratitude is the beginning of what we seek and the fulfillment of who we want to be.

Q *How can a person detect a diminished*
sense of gratitude in his or her life?

A There are two ways: First, unhappiness. Gratitude supplies
the energy and provides the reason to be happy. We tend to be
happy in proportion to our being grateful. If people were asked
to separately rate themselves on happiness and gratefulness
using a rating scale, I suspect the number would be about the
same for both. Happiness and gratitude belong together. The
words are almost interchangeable ways to express a positive
outlook on life. They are symbiotically related; one serves
the other and vice versa. Grateful people are happy people;
seldom is one grateful and unhappy.

Second, selfishness. Gratitude wants to do something to
contribute to the happiness of others. Being service-oriented,
it seeks ways to give itself away, using its resources as an
instrument for doing good. Happy people are grateful people;
seldom are grateful people selfish.

Questions for Journaling or Group Discussion Sessions

What is Gratitude?

1. What are the outward signs of gratitude's role in your life?

2. Identify and briefly describe a gratitude-filled event in your life.

3. How do you typically express your gratitude?

4. How do you see gratitude being played out in other people's stories?

5. What do you want from life that would increase your experience of gratitude?

6. What would your life look/feel like if more people were grateful for what you do?

7. How can you overcome the pressure to make gratitude a social obligation rather than a blessing of joyous giving?

Uses and benefits of gratitude

8. How can gratitude be a gateway for viewing, redirecting, and rejuvenating life?

9. How is gratitude a way to simplify life and surrender our endless desire for more?

10. How can gratitude help one revisit good times to deal with the inevitable adversity and losses in life?

11. How has ingratitude contributed to bouts of discontent and disillusionment?

12. How can you use gratitude to face and resolve some of the demands and conflicts in your life?

13. How does undue attention to your shortcomings and setbacks in life undermine your experiences of gratitude?

14. Identify a reversal in life, an unfortunate or unexpected turn of events that you look back upon with gratitude today.

How to become more grateful

15. List four things you can do to make gratitude an intentional way of living.

16. What can you do to make gratitude an organizing force in your life?

17. What differences do you note in your feelings expressing gratitude in various ways?

18. How can gratitude be interwoven with other virtues to set one's course in life?

19. What do you need to write into the story of your life to breathe more gratitude into it?

20. How has gratitude been a source of healing in your life?

21. Life generally involves some kind of sacrifice. Name a couple of sacrifices you have made and/or have been made on your behalf that have resulted in gratitude.

22. What are the obstacles to being or becoming a more grateful person?

23. How has gratitude deepened and increased your generosity to others?

24. How has gratitude for the people in your life helped you deal with the transitory pleasure derived from material goods?

25. What questions about gratitude remain unanswered after reading this book?